HOW TO FIND PURPOSE IN LIFE

A Journey of Self-Discovery and Meaningful Living

JERRY ROBERT

ACKNOWLEDGEMENT

I would like to express my deepest gratitude to my family and friends, Whose unwavering support and love have fueled my own pursuit of purpose. Special thanks to the countless individuals whose stories have inspired me, And to the mentors who have guided me along this transformative path.

TABLE OF CONTENTS

CHAPTER ONE

Unveilling the Essence of Purpose

CHAPTER TWO

Navigating the Inner Landscape

I. Exploring Your Passions and Talents

II. Understanding Your Core Values

III. Reflecting on Your Life's Journey

CHAPTER THREE

Embracing the Power of Intuition

I. Tuning into Your Inner Voice

II. Cultivating Intuitive Decision-Making

CHAPTER FOUR

Cultivating Authenticity

I. Embracing Your True Self

II. Overcoming Self-Doubt and Fear of Judgment

III. Honouring Your Unique Path

CHAPTER FIVE

Aligning Values and Actions

I. Discovering Your Core Values

II. Living in Alignment with Your Values

III. Creating Meaningful Goals and Intentions

CHAPTER SIX

Connecting with Others and Contributing to the World

I. Building Authentic Relationships

II. Discovering Your Unique Contribution

III. Making a Positive Impact

CHAPTER SEVEN

Resilience and the Pursuit of Purpose

I. Navigating Setbacks and Obstacles

II. Building Resilience in the Face of Adversity

III. Persevering on the Path of Purpose

CHAPTER EIGHT

Embracing Imperfections and Finding Gratitude

CHAPTER NINE

Heal with Forgiveness & Compassion

CHAPTER TEN

Gratitude Mindset Journey

CONCLUSION

RECOMMENDED BOOKS

INTRODUCTION

In a world brimming with distractions and uncertainties, finding purpose has become a pressing quest for many. This book aims to serve as a compass, gently guiding you towards the discovery of your life's purpose. Through introspection, exploration, and timeless wisdom, we will embark on a transformative journey together, unravelling the secrets of fulfillment and meaning. Prepare to delve into the depths of your soul, embrace the challenges that lie ahead, and emerge with a profound understanding of how to infuse your life with purpose.

CHAPTER ONE

Unveilling the Essence of Purpose

"The only limit to our realization of tomorrow will be our doubts of today." - Franklin D. Roosevelt

Purpose—the very word carries a weight and significance that resonates deeply within the human spirit. It is an intangible force that propels us forward, guides our actions, and gives meaning to our existence. But what is the essence of purpose? How do we uncover its true nature and harness its power to lead fulfilling lives? At its core, purpose is the driving force behind our actions, the compass that directs our choices and shapes our destiny. It is not a mere goal or objective but a profound understanding of why we do what we do and the impact we seek to make in the world. Purpose emerges from a deep exploration of our values, passions, and unique gifts, as well as a genuine desire to contribute to something greater than ourselves. To unveil the essence of purpose, we must embark on a journey of self-discovery—a process of introspection and reflection that delves into the depths of our being. It requires us to ask ourselves profound questions: What brings us joy and fulfillment? What are our core values and beliefs? What are the innate talents and strengths we possess? By exploring these facets of our identity, we begin to unravel the threads that weave together our purpose. In our search for purpose, we often encounter the whispers of our intuition—the inner voice that guides us towards our authentic selves. Listening to this voice requires quieting the noise of external expectations and societal pressures. It calls for solitude, stillness, and a willingness to embrace the unknown. By attuning ourselves to our intuition, we gain access to a wellspring of wisdom that can lead us to our true calling. Moreover, purpose is not a fixed destination but a dynamic and evolving process. It may reveal itself in unexpected ways and shift as we grow and change. Embracing the fluid nature of purpose allows us to adapt and navigate the twists and turns of life's journey. It invites us to stay open-minded, remain curious, and be receptive to the lessons and opportunities that come our way. Unveiling the essence of purpose also requires action—a willingness to take risks, step out of our comfort zones, and pursue our dreams with unwavering determination. Purpose without action is but a beautiful concept, lost in the realm of possibility. We must be willing to translate our aspirations into tangible steps, aligning our thoughts, words, and deeds with the vision we hold within. However, purpose is not solely about personal fulfillment. It extends beyond the boundaries of the self and embraces a broader sense of interconnectedness. When we uncover our purpose, we begin to understand that our individual journey is intricately intertwined with the well-being of others and the world at large. Purpose becomes a force for positive change—a catalyst for creating a more compassionate, just, and sustainable future. Ultimately, unveiling the essence of purpose is an ongoing process—a lifelong quest that demands our constant attention and commitment. It requires courage, resilience, and a willingness to embrace both the light and shadow aspects of our existence. In the face of adversity and uncertainty, purpose provides us with an anchor—a guiding light that helps us navigate the storms and find meaning amidst the chaos. As we embark on this journey of self-discovery, let us remember that purpose is not a destination to be reached but a path to be walked. It is not something we find but something we cultivate within ourselves. By honouring our values, following our passions, and embracing our unique gifts, we unveil the essence of purpose and embark on a transformative voyage that enriches not only our lives but also the lives of those around us. In the end, purpose is the heartbeat of our existence—the thread that weaves together the tapestry of our lives. It is the spark that ignites our souls, propels us towards greatness, and empowers us to leave a lasting impact on the world. Unveiling the essence of purpose is an invitation to live authentically, to live with intention, and to embark on a remarkable journey of self-discovery and self-actualization.

Now, pay close attention to these key points as you embark on the journey of unveiling the essence of purpose. Take the time for self-exploration, delving into your values, passions, and unique gifts. This is where your purpose begins to unfold.
Trust your intuition and listen closely to your inner voice. They will serve as your guides, leading you towards your authentic self and purpose. Remember that purpose is not fixed; it evolves and changes over time. Embrace the fluidity and stay open to new possibilities that may arise. Be courageous and take action. Pursue your dreams with unwavering determination, even if it means stepping out of your comfort zone and taking risks. Recognize the broader impact of your purpose. It goes beyond personal fulfillment and encompasses making a positive difference in the lives of others and the world. Understand that unveiling the essence of purpose is a lifelong journey. Continuously reflect, grow, and adapt as you discover new layers of meaning. Embrace the transformative power of this journey. Unveiling the essence of purpose will not only enrich your life but also inspire and impact those around you. Live authentically and with intention. Let your purpose shine through your choices, embracing who you truly are and what you aim to achieve. Embrace purpose as a guiding light during challenging times. It provides meaning and acts as an anchor, helping you navigate through adversity.
These key points will serve as a roadmap as you embark on this remarkable voyage of self-discovery and self-actualization. Keep them in mind as you explore the depths of your purpose.

Once upon a time, in a small town, there lived a young man named George Bush. From a young age, George felt a deep longing for something more—a yearning to uncover the essence of his purpose. He was determined to embark on a transformative journey of self-discovery. George's quest began with introspection and reflection. He spent countless hours exploring his values, passions, and unique gifts. His love for people and desire to make a positive impact in their lives fueled his search. He realized that his purpose resided in serving others and making a difference on a grand scale. With clarity in mind, George listened attentively to his inner voice and trusted his intuition. He understood that his purpose would not be handed to him on a silver platter but required courage and action. George set out to take risks, step out of his comfort zone, and pursue his dreams with unwavering determination. Throughout his journey, George encountered numerous obstacles and faced moments of self-doubt. However, he embraced resilience as a guiding principle. Every setback became an opportunity for growth, and he learned to persevere with unwavering faith in his purpose. George also understood the importance of authenticity. He stayed true to himself, aligning his purpose with his core values, never compromising his integrity. This authenticity fueled his connection with others, and he fostered compassion and kindness along his path. As George's purpose began to take shape, he experienced the profound impact of collaboration. He sought out like-minded individuals who shared his vision, forming partnerships that amplified his purpose and expanded his reach. Through collective efforts, George realized that his purpose was not solely his own; it was a shared journey towards a brighter future. George recognized the significance of leaving a lasting legacy. He understood that his purpose extended beyond his lifetime, and he wanted to create positive change for future generations. He cultivated a growth mindset, viewing failures as opportunities for learning and progress. With humility and gratitude, he remained committed to continuous self-improvement and growth. As George's purpose unfolded, he never forgot the importance of self-care. He realized that nurturing his own well-being was essential to sustaining his energy and impact. By practicing self-care, he replenished his spirit and became an even greater force for good. Through his unwavering dedication, George Bush unveiled the true essence of his purpose. His journey was not without its challenges, but he emerged as a beacon of inspiration, guiding others towards their own paths of purpose. George's story reminds us that we all have the power to unveil the essence of our purpose. By embarking on a journey of self-discovery, embracing authenticity, resilience, collaboration, and self-care, we can find our own unique purpose and make a lasting impact in the world. And so, George's legacy lives on, inspiring generations to come, as he showed us the transformative power of unveiling the essence of purpose.

Certainly! Here are some principles to write down when it comes to unveiling the essence of purpose:
- **Authenticity:** Embrace your true self and align your purpose with your genuine values, passions, and beliefs.
- **Clarity:** Seek clarity by reflecting on your aspirations, goals, and the impact you wish to create in the world.
- **Intentionality:** Live with intention, making deliberate choices that align with your purpose and contribute to your growth.
- **Legacy:** Consider the long-term impact of your purpose and how it can create a positive and lasting legacy for future generations.
- **Growth mindset:** Embrace a growth mindset, seeing failures and setbacks as learning experiences that propel you forward.

Write down these principles and let them serve as guiding lights on your purposeful journey. They will remind you of the core values and mindset needed to unveil the true essence of your purpose and make a meaningful impact in your life and the world around you.

Unveiling the essence of purpose is a profound and transformative journey that leads us to a life of fulfillment, meaning, and impact. It is a journey that requires introspection, reflection, and the willingness to listen to our inner voice.

As we delve into the depths of our being, exploring our values, passions, and unique gifts, our purpose begins to take shape. It is not a fixed destination, but a dynamic and evolving process that adapts as we grow and change. Purpose is not solely about personal fulfillment; it extends beyond ourselves and encompasses making a positive impact on others and the world. It calls for action, courage, and collaboration to bring our aspirations into reality.

The journey of unveiling the essence of purpose is not without its challenges. It demands resilience, authenticity, and a growth mindset. It requires us to embrace failures as stepping stones toward growth and to practice self-care to sustain our energy and well-being along the way. Ultimately, by embracing our purpose and aligning our thoughts, words, and actions with our values, we become catalysts for positive change. We leave a lasting legacy, inspiring others to embark on their own journeys of self-discovery and purpose. So, let us embark on this remarkable voyage of self-discovery, guided by the principles of authenticity, clarity, resilience, compassion, and collaboration. By unveiling the essence of our purpose, we unlock the power within us to make a profound impact and create a better world for ourselves and future generations. May we embrace this journey with open hearts and unwavering determination, knowing that our purpose is not a destination but a path to be walked, an ever-unfolding story that shapes our lives and the lives of those around us.

CHAPTER TWO

Navigating the Inner Landscape

"Don't watch the clock; do what it does. Keep going." - Sam Levenson

Sam Levenson was born on December 28, 1911, in New York City. He grew up in a modest Jewish immigrant family in Brooklyn, where he developed a sharp wit and a love for storytelling. Sam's parents instilled in him the importance of education and hard work. From a young age, Sam showed exceptional intelligence and a natural talent for public speaking. He excelled in school and developed a passion for literature and writing. Sam's ability to captivate audiences with his words became evident during his high school years when he joined the debate team. After graduating from high school, Sam pursued higher education at City College of New York. He studied English and speech, honing his skills as a writer and speaker. During this time, he also began performing in local theatre productions, further refining his stage presence and comedic timing. Sam's talent for storytelling led him to explore opportunities in radio and television. In the 1940s and 1950s, he became a popular radio personality, known for his humorous anecdotes and witty observations about everyday life. His unique blend of humour and relatability resonated with audiences, making him a beloved figure in the entertainment industry. In the late 1950s, Sam began appearing on television, making regular appearances on popular shows like "The Ed Sullivan Show" and "The Tonight Show Starring Johnny Carson." His comedic storytelling and quick wit earned him a significant following and established him as a prominent figure in the world of entertainment. Sam Levenson's success on television catapulted him into the realm of writing. He authored several books, including "In One Era and Out the Other" and "You Don't Have to Be in Who's Who to Know What's What." His books, filled with humorous and insightful reflections on life, resonated with readers across generations. Throughout his career, Sam Levenson remained dedicated to education. He recognized the importance of inspiring and empowering young minds, and he became a prominent advocate for quality education. Sam delivered motivational speeches to teachers and students, emphasizing the value of knowledge, perseverance, and self-belief. Sam Levenson's legacy extends beyond his accomplishments as an entertainer and author. He touched the lives of many through his wit, wisdom, and ability to find humour in everyday situations. Sam's stories continue to inspire and entertain people around the world, reminding us of the power of laughter, resilience, and the joy of sharing our experiences. Sam passed away on August 27, 1980, but his influence lives on through his timeless writings, recordings, and the memories of those who were fortunate enough to experience his wit and wisdom firsthand. His dedication to education and his ability to bring laughter into the lives of others continue to make him a beloved figure and an enduring source of inspiration. In conclusion, Sam Levenson was a remarkable individual who left a lasting impact through his talent for storytelling, humour, and dedication to education. His ability to connect with audiences through his words and bring joy to people's lives made him a beloved figure in the entertainment industry. Sam's journey from a humble immigrant family in Brooklyn to becoming a renowned radio and television personality exemplifies the power of hard work, determination, and a passion for one's craft. He used his platform to not only entertain but also inspire others to pursue their dreams and embrace the value of education. Through his books, speeches, and performances, Sam Levenson touched the hearts of many, reminding us to find humour in life's challenges and to never underestimate the power of laughter. His legacy continues to resonate with people across generations, serving as a reminder to embrace our unique stories and share them with the world. Sam Levenson's contributions to literature, entertainment, and education have left an indelible mark. His wit, wisdom, and ability to connect with others will continue to inspire and uplift countless individuals for years to come. His story serves as a reminder that with passion, perseverance, and a genuine desire to make a difference, we too can leave a lasting legacy and bring joy to others through our own unique talents.

The human experience is a vast and intricate tapestry, woven with the threads of thoughts, emotions, and perceptions. While the external world captures our attention with its myriad of distractions and demands, it is the inner landscape that holds the key to understanding ourselves and finding meaning in our lives. Navigating this inner terrain is a profound journey of self-discovery, requiring curiosity, courage, and introspection. The inner landscape is a realm that exists within each of us—a rich tapestry of thoughts, feelings, memories, and beliefs. It is the fertile ground upon which our experiences are processed, interpreted, and given meaning. Just as a map guides us through uncharted territories, exploring the inner landscape requires us to develop a keen sense of self-awareness and a willingness to delve into the depths of our psyche. As we venture deeper into the inner landscape, we may encounter emotional terrains that are uncomfortable or unfamiliar. It is here that emotional intelligence comes into play—a capacity to recognize, understand, and manage our emotions effectively. Embracing the full spectrum of our emotions, from joy and love to fear and sadness, allows us to navigate through the complexities of our internal landscape with greater ease and authenticity. By acknowledging and honouring our emotions, we can learn valuable lessons about ourselves and cultivate emotional resilience. Another essential aspect of navigating the inner landscape is exploring our core values and beliefs. Our values serve as a compass, guiding our choices and actions. Reflecting on what truly matters to us helps us align our lives with our deepest convictions. By examining our beliefs, we can uncover any limiting or outdated ones that may hinder our personal growth. This process of introspection enables us to make conscious choices that are in harmony with our authentic selves, leading to a more fulfilling and purposeful existence. Navigating the inner landscape also involves engaging in practices that foster self-reflection and self-expression. Journaling, meditation, creative pursuits, and therapy are just a few examples of activities that can facilitate this process. These practices provide us with a space for introspection, allowing thoughts and feelings to surface and be explored. Through self-expression, we give voice to our innermost experiences, gaining clarity and insight into our own narratives. It is important to note that navigating the inner landscape is not a linear journey. Just as rivers wind and change course, our inner world can be fluid and dynamic. Growth and transformation are constant companions on this expedition. We must be open to embracing change, embracing the discomfort that often accompanies it. By surrendering to the ebb and flow of life, we create the conditions for profound personal evolution. In navigating the inner landscape, it is crucial to cultivate self-compassion and kindness. We are complex beings with strengths and vulnerabilities, and our journey may be marked by setbacks, challenges, and moments of self-doubt. Embracing ourselves with compassion, offering understanding and forgiveness, allows us to move forward with resilience and grace. Ultimately, navigating the inner landscape is a deeply personal and transformative endeavour. It is an invitation to embark on a lifelong exploration of self, peering into the depths of our being with curiosity and compassion. By embracing the richness and complexity of our inner world, we unlock the potential for growth, healing, and self-actualization. As we navigate our inner landscape, we come to realize that the truest and most profound discoveries lie within ourselves. Navigating the inner landscape is a fascinating topic for brainstorming. Let's dive into it and explore some important points. Here are a few to get us started:

INTUITION AND INNER WISDOM:

Intuition and inner wisdom are indeed fascinating aspects of navigating the inner landscape. They can serve as powerful guides on your journey of self-discovery and personal growth. Intuition is often described as our inner knowing, a deep-seated sense of understanding or insight that arises without conscious reasoning. It's an intuitive sense that goes beyond logical analysis and taps into our subconscious wisdom. When you trust your intuition, we are open to receiving information that may not be readily apparent on the surface. Developing and honing your intuition involves cultivating a sense of attunement with yourself. It requires creating space for stillness and silence, allowing you to listen to the whispers of your inner voice. Practices like meditation, mindfulness, or simply quiet reflection can help you tune in and become more receptive to your intuition. Inner wisdom, on the other hand, encompasses the reservoir of knowledge and understanding that resides within you. It arises from a combination of your life experiences, insights, and a deep connection to your authentic selves. Your inner wisdom guides us in making choices that align with your values and purpose. Accessing your inner wisdom often involves slowing down and creating space for reflection. It means pausing amidst the busyness of life to listen to the wisdom that emerges from within. This can be done through journaling, engaging in meaningful conversations, or seeking solitude in nature. Trusting your intuition and tapping into your inner wisdom can bring numerous benefits. They can help you make decisions aligned with your true selves, navigate challenging situations with greater clarity, and find deeper meaning and purpose in your life. It's important to note that developing your intuition and accessing your inner wisdom is an ongoing practice that requires patience, self-trust, and a willingness to listen deeply. Have you had any experiences where you felt connected to your intuition or tapped into your inner wisdom? How do you personally cultivate these aspects in your own journey of navigating the inner landscape? Let's further explore and discuss your insights on intuition and inner wisdom.

Practices such as meditation, mindfulness, and deep breathing exercises can help quiet the mind and increase your receptivity to intuitive insights. Engaging in activities that bring you joy and a sense of flow can also help you connect with your intuition, as it often speaks to you through a sense of resonance and alignment. Additionally, paying attention to your body's wisdom can provide valuable insights. Your body often carries messages and sensations that convey important information. Developing somatic awareness, such as noticing tension or sensations in different parts of the body, can help you tap into your inner wisdom and gain a deeper understanding of yourself. As you cultivate your intuition and connect with your inner wisdom, it's essential to approach them with openness and discernment. Sometimes, intuitive messages may challenge your existing beliefs or require you to step outside your comfort zones. It's important to discern whether the guidance comes from a place of fear or ego, or if it aligns with your authentic selves and serves your highest good. By cultivating your intuition and connecting with your inner wisdom, you can navigate the inner landscape with greater clarity, purpose, and alignment. These aspects can serve as valuable compasses, guide you on your journey of self-discovery and help you make choices that resonate with your true self.

PERSONAL RITUALS AND SACRED SPACES:

Personal rituals and sacred spaces are significant aspects of navigating the inner landscape. They provide a framework for self-reflection, introspection, and connection to your deeper self. Let's delve into it.

Personal rituals are intentional practices that hold meaning and significance for you. They can be simple or elaborate, depending on personal preference. Rituals provide a sense of structure and sacredness, allowing you to engage in activities that nourish your soul and promote self-awareness.

These rituals can take various forms, such as daily meditation or mindfulness practices, journaling, setting intentions, engaging in creative activities, or even having a sacred morning or evening routine. The key is to infuse these practices with mindfulness and intention, creating a dedicated space and time for self-care, reflection, and inner exploration.

Sacred spaces are physical or metaphorical environments that we create or designate as places of refuge, tranquillity, and connection. They are spaces where we can retreat and engage in practices that foster inner growth. A sacred space can be a designated corner in our home, a natural setting, a meditation cushion, or even a virtual space that holds personal significance.

In these sacred spaces, we can engage in rituals, meditate, pray, or simply be present with ourselves. They provide a sanctuary where we can detach from the external noise and reconnect with our inner landscape. Creating a sacred space allows us to cultivate a deeper connection to ourselves and the spiritual dimensions of our lives.

The ambiance and elements within a sacred space are unique to each individual. Some may incorporate candles, incense, or meaningful objects like crystals, images, or sacred texts. Others may prefer simplicity, with emphasis on quiet and minimalism. The intention is to create an environment that fosters a sense of calm, introspection, and reverence.

Engaging in personal rituals and cultivating sacred spaces encourages a deeper connection with our inner selves and the present moment. They serve as reminders to prioritize self-care, self-reflection, and personal growth. Rituals and sacred spaces also provide a sense of stability and grounding in an ever-changing world, allowing us to access a space of inner stillness and wisdom.

Do you have any personal rituals or sacred spaces that you incorporate into your journey of navigating the inner landscape? How do they support your self-discovery and well-being? Think about these questions for a moment and write down your answers. The world is controlled by infinite intelligence and that's why you have to meditate frequently.

EMBODIMENT AND SOMATIC AWARENESS:

Embodiment and somatic awareness are essential elements in the journey of navigating the inner landscape. They involve deepening our connection with our physical bodies and developing an awareness of the sensations, emotions, and wisdom that arise within us.

Embodiment refers to the process of fully inhabiting and being present in our physical bodies. In our fast-paced and often disembodied society, it's common to become disconnected from our bodies and live predominantly in our minds. However, true self-discovery and inner growth require a holistic integration of the mind, body, and spirit.

By cultivating embodiment, we become attuned to the messages and wisdom that our bodies offer. We start to recognize the physical sensations that accompany our emotions, thoughts, and experiences. This heightened awareness allows us to access a deeper level of self-understanding and authenticity.

Somatic awareness goes hand in hand with embodiment. It involves tuning into the sensations, movements, and subtle energy within our bodies. Somatic practices invite us to explore the felt sense of our experiences, bypassing intellectual analysis and tapping into the wisdom of our bodies.

There are various practices that can support embodiment and somatic awareness. Mindful movement practices like yoga, tai chi, or dance can help us reconnect with our bodies and develop a greater sense of embodiment. These practices encourage us to be fully present, to listen to the sensations in our bodies, and to honour our physical boundaries and needs. Additionally, body scan meditations can be helpful in developing somatic awareness. By systematically bringing attention to different parts of the body, we cultivate a deeper understanding of the sensations and emotions held within. Breathwork exercises and progressive muscle relaxation techniques can also enhance somatic awareness and promote a sense of relaxation and embodiment.

Embodiment and somatic awareness enable us to access deeper layers of our being. They provide a doorway to unravelling unconscious patterns, healing emotional wounds, and integrating mind-body-spirit connections. Through this process, we develop a more compassionate and nurturing relationship with our bodies, enhancing our overall well-being and self-discovery.

CULTIVATING CURIOSITY:

Cultivating curiosity is a powerful mindset and approach that can greatly enhance the journey of navigating the inner landscape. When we approach ourselves and the world with genuine curiosity, we open doors to new possibilities, insights, and personal growth.

Curiosity is the innate desire to explore, question, and seek understanding. It is the fuel that drives us to inquire, learn, and discover. When we cultivate curiosity, we invite a sense of wonder and openness into our lives, enabling us to engage with the inner landscape in a more profound way.

Cultivating curiosity within the context of navigating the inner landscape involves a willingness to explore and inquire into our thoughts, emotions, beliefs, and experiences. It means approaching ourselves with a sense of wonder, even in moments of discomfort or uncertainty. Rather than being judgmental or rigid, we adopt a mindset of curiosity that allows for growth, learning, and self-discovery.

Curiosity encourages us to ask questions, challenge assumptions, and explore different perspectives. It prompts us to seek deeper insights and understanding about ourselves, our motivations, and the patterns that shape our lives. By embracing curiosity, we become active participants in our inner journey, continually seeking to uncover new layers of self-awareness and meaning.

Practices that foster curiosity can include journaling, self-reflection exercises, or engaging in meaningful conversations with others. These activities invite us to delve into our inner landscape, inquire into our experiences, and embrace the unknown. They encourage us to question our beliefs, assumptions, and narratives, creating space for personal growth and transformation.

Cultivating curiosity also involves embracing the concept of "beginner's mind," approaching each moment with a fresh perspective and a sense of openness. It means letting go of preconceived notions and being willing to explore the uncharted territories of our inner world with a sense of curiosity and adventure.

By cultivating curiosity, we invite a sense of discovery, growth, and expansion into our lives. It allows us to tap into our innate creativity, explore new possibilities, and foster a deeper connection with ourselves. Curiosity empowers us to navigate the inner landscape with an open heart and an inquisitive mind.

SHADOW WORK:

Shadow work is a profound and transformative process within the realm of navigating the inner landscape. It involves exploring and integrating the aspects of ourselves that we may have repressed, denied, or considered undesirable—the shadow.

The shadow, as described by Carl Jung, represents the unconscious parts of ourselves that contain unacknowledged emotions, desires, and traits. These aspects often arise from societal conditioning, past experiences, or parts of our personalities that we have disowned or rejected.

Engaging in shadow work requires courage, self-compassion, and a willingness to delve into the depths of our psyche. By shining a light on our shadow, we can uncover hidden beliefs, patterns, and wounds that impact our thoughts, emotions, and behaviors.

Shadow work often involves self-reflection, introspection, and honest exploration of our shadow aspects. Journaling can be a valuable tool in this process, allowing us to bring awareness to the shadow elements and gain insight into their origins and effects on our lives. Engaging in therapy or working with a trained professional can also provide guidance and support in navigating the complexities of shadow work.

The purpose of shadow work is not to eliminate or suppress these shadow aspects, but rather to integrate and understand them. By embracing and accepting our shadow, we move towards wholeness and self-acceptance. It allows us to reclaim parts of ourselves that have been neglected, leading to greater authenticity, inner harmony, and personal growth.

Shadow work can be challenging and may bring up uncomfortable emotions, but it offers profound rewards. It helps us dismantle limiting beliefs, heal emotional wounds, and cultivate compassion for ourselves and others. It also empowers us to make conscious choices and break free from unconscious patterns that no longer serve us.

It's important to approach shadow work with self-care and support. Creating a safe and nurturing environment, seeking guidance from professionals, and practicing self-compassion are crucial aspects of this journey. Remember that shadow work is a process that unfolds over time, and it requires patience, vulnerability, and a commitment to self-discovery.

Navigating the inner landscape is a deeply personal and ongoing journey that involves exploring and understanding one's own thoughts, emotions, beliefs, and desires. It is a process of self-discovery and self-awareness that can lead to personal growth, healing, and transformation.

Throughout this chapter, it becomes evident that the inner landscape is complex and multifaceted. It is influenced by a variety of factors, including past experiences, cultural and societal influences, personal values, and external circumstances. It is a dynamic terrain that is constantly evolving and responding to internal and external stimuli.

To navigate the inner landscape effectively, it is important to cultivate self-awareness, which involves observing and acknowledging one's thoughts, emotions, and patterns of behavior without judgement. This awareness allows individuals to gain insight into their own inner workings, recognize unhealthy patterns or beliefs, and make conscious choices that align with their authentic selves.

Developing practices such as mindfulness, meditation, journaling, or therapy can provide valuable tools for navigating the inner landscape. These practices help individuals develop a deeper connection with themselves, tune into their intuition, and cultivate a sense of inner peace and balance.

It is essential to approach the inner landscape with curiosity, compassion, and patience. It is not a linear process, and setbacks or challenges are to be expected. Navigating the inner landscape requires a willingness to face and explore uncomfortable emotions and beliefs, as well as a commitment to personal growth and self-improvement.

Ultimately, the journey through the inner landscape is a lifelong endeavour. It is not about reaching a final destination but rather embracing the process of self-discovery and embracing the full range of one's experiences and emotions. Through this chapter, individuals can cultivate a deeper understanding of themselves, develop meaningful relationships with others, and live a more authentic and fulfilling life. Now let's look at the importance of exploring your passions and talents.

I.   Exploring Your Passions and Talents

Discovering and nurturing your passions and talents is a transformative journey that can bring immense joy, fulfillment, and success to your life. Each person possesses a unique combination of interests and innate abilities waiting to be explored. By embarking on this exploration, you unlock the potential to lead a more purposeful and meaningful existence. In this article, we will delve into the importance of exploring your passions and talents and provide you with some relevant self-questions to guide you along this rewarding path.

Passions and talents are intrinsically linked to your sense of identity and purpose. Your passions are the activities, subjects, or causes that ignite your enthusiasm, fuel your motivation, and bring you deep satisfaction. Talents, on the other hand, are the innate skills and abilities that come naturally to you and can be honed and developed over time. Combining your passions and talents enables you to excel in areas that resonate with your authentic self, leading to a more gratifying and successful life.

Here are some pertinent questions to examine if you need to investigate the significance of pursuing your passions and talents.

1. What hobbies or interests have you always been drawn to?
2. What do you enjoy learning about or discussing with others?
3. What skills or activities come naturally to you?
4. What dreams and aspirations have you held since childhood?
5. What activities bring you a sense of fulfillment and purpose?

Once you've identified your passions and talents through self-questioning, it's essential to embrace the exploration process. Experiment with different activities and opportunities that align with your identified interests. Engage in courses, workshops, and community involvement to further develop your skills and expand your knowledge. Embrace challenges as opportunities for growth and view setbacks as valuable learning experiences. Remember, the journey itself is as important as the destination.

Exploring your passions and talents is a transformative endeavour that leads to a more fulfilling and purpose-driven life. By answering relevant self-questions and embarking on the journey of self-discovery, you unlock your unique potential and open doors to endless possibilities. Embrace the exploration process, pursue your passions, and nurture your talents, as they are the keys to living a life brimming with joy, meaning, and success.

Exploring your passions and talents is of paramount importance for personal growth, fulfillment, and overall well-being. Here are some key reasons why it is crucial to embark on this journey:

1. **Discovering your purpose:** Exploring your passions and talents allows you to discover your true purpose in life. When you engage in activities that align with your passions, you experience a sense of meaning and fulfillment. Understanding your purpose provides a guiding light, helping you make choices and decisions that resonate with your authentic self.
2. **Enhanced self-awareness:** Exploring your passions and talents deepens your self-awareness. It allows you to understand your strengths, weaknesses, values, and desires on a profound level. This self-awareness helps you make informed decisions, set meaningful goals, and cultivate a stronger sense of identity.
3. **Increased motivation and engagement:** When you engage in activities you are passionate about and utilize your talents, you naturally experience higher levels of motivation and engagement. Time flies by, and you enter a state of flow where your skills are fully utilized, leading to a sense of joy and fulfillment. This heightened motivation and engagement contribute to higher productivity and success in your endeavours.
4. Building resilience and perseverance: **The journey of explor**ing your passions and talents often comes with challenges and setbacks. However, these obstacles provide valuable opportunities for growth and development. By facing and overcoming these challenges, you build resilience, perseverance, and a stronger character. These qualities will serve you well in all areas of life.

Exploring your passions and talents is not only important for personal growth but also for leading a fulfilling and purpose-driven life. By understanding yourself on a deeper level, embracing your strengths, and pursuing what truly matters to you, you unlock your potential, experience higher levels of engagement and fulfillment, and inspire those around you. Embrace the journey of self-discovery, and let your passions and talents guide you towards a life of meaning and joy.

II. Understanding Your Core Values

Core values are the fundamental beliefs and principles that guide our behavior and decision-making. They are the essence of who we are as individuals and serve as a compass in navigating life's choices. Understanding your core values is crucial because they shape your attitudes, actions, and priorities. By identifying and aligning with your core values, you gain clarity, purpose, and a strong foundation for living a fulfilling and authentic life. In this page, we will explore the importance of understanding your core values and how they can positively impact various aspects of your life.

Firstly, understanding your core values allows you to make decisions that are in alignment with your authentic self. When you are clear about what truly matters to you, it becomes easier to choose paths that resonate with your values. Whether it's selecting a career, forming relationships, or pursuing personal goals, your core values provide a framework for evaluating options and making choices that are consistent with who you are at your core. This alignment promotes a sense of authenticity, leading to increased self-confidence and fulfillment.

Moreover, core values act as a source of motivation and drive. When your actions and goals are aligned with your values, you are more likely to experience a deep sense of purpose and passion. Your values become a source of inspiration, fueling your commitment and perseverance. For example, if one of your core values is environmental sustainability, you might feel motivated to adopt a sustainable lifestyle, participate in conservation efforts, or work for an eco-friendly company. By connecting your goals and aspirations with your core values, you tap into a wellspring of inner motivation that propels you forward.

Understanding your core values also helps in establishing healthy boundaries. When you are aware of what you stand for, it becomes easier to define your limits and protect your well-being. Core values provide a moral compass, guiding you in determining what is acceptable and unacceptable in various situations. For instance, if honesty is one of your core values, you are more likely to prioritize open communication and refrain from engaging in deceitful behavior. By establishing boundaries based on your values, you create a framework for healthy relationships and self-respect.

Furthermore, core values play a vital role in cultivating a sense of self-awareness. Exploring and understanding your values requires introspection and reflection. It prompts you to evaluate your beliefs, examine your priorities, and gain a deeper understanding of what truly matters to you. This process of self-discovery enhances self-awareness and helps you become more attuned to your thoughts, emotions, and desires. As a result, you develop a stronger sense of identity and can navigate life's challenges with greater clarity and resilience.

Understanding your core values also aids in prioritizing your time and energy. When you have a clear understanding of what is truly important to you, you can allocate your resources accordingly. By aligning your actions with your values, you avoid wasting time on activities or relationships that do not contribute to your well-being or personal growth. This focused approach enables you to make the most of your limited time and energy, leading to a more balanced and fulfilling life.

Napoleon had always been curious about the world around him and possessed an insatiable hunger for knowledge. He was particularly fascinated by the concept of success and the factors that contributed to achieving it.

As he grew older, Napoleon embarked on a journey of self-discovery and personal development. He dove into books, attended seminars, and sought out mentors who could guide him along his path. During his quest, he stumbled upon the concept of core values—a profound revelation that would forever change his life.

Napoleon began to delve deep into his own soul, contemplating his beliefs, aspirations, and principles. He asked himself, "What truly matters to me? What do I stand for? What are the guiding principles that I want to shape my life around?" These questions ignited a fire within him, driving him to explore his core values with unwavering determination.

Through introspection and reflection, Napoleon discovered that one of his core values was integrity. He realized that he wanted to live a life of honesty, transparency, and ethical behavior. This revelation became the foundation upon which he built his character and made his decisions. With integrity as his guiding light, Napoleon knew that he would never compromise his principles or engage in dishonest practices, no matter the circumstances. Another core value that Napoleon identified was personal growth. He had an unyielding desire to continuously learn, improve, and evolve. Napoleon understood that growth was the key to unlocking his true potential and achieving his dreams. With this value at the forefront of his mind, he dedicated himself to lifelong learning, seeking out opportunities to expand his knowledge, develop new skills, and challenge himself beyond his comfort zone.

Napoleon also discovered that he held a deep-seated value for helping others. He believed in the power of lifting people up, inspiring them, and making a positive impact in their lives. This realization ignited his passion for writing and speaking, as he saw these mediums as vehicles to share his knowledge and empower others to reach their own greatness.

As Napoleon continued to embrace and embody his core values, his life began to transform. He found himself making decisions with clarity and conviction, unafraid to pursue his dreams and overcome obstacles. His commitment to integrity allowed him to build trust and forge meaningful connections with others, creating a strong support network that propelled him forward.

The value of personal growth drove Napoleon to achieve remarkable feats. He became a renowned author, captivating audiences with his writings on success, motivation, and self-improvement. His commitment to helping others led him to develop courses and seminars that empowered countless individuals to realize their full potential and achieve their own versions of success.

Napoleon Hill's journey of understanding his core values not only shaped his life but also left an indelible mark on the world. His unwavering commitment to integrity, personal growth, and helping others became a legacy that continues to inspire generations to this day.
Understanding Core Values: Key Principles:

1. NON-JUDGEMENT:

Non-judgment is an important principle when it comes to understanding core values and interacting with others. It involves approaching different perspectives, beliefs, and values without imposing our own judgments or evaluations upon them. Non-judgment allows us to embrace diversity, foster understanding, and create a space for open-mindedness and acceptance.

When practicing non-judgment, we suspend our preconceived notions and biases, avoiding the tendency to label or categorize others based on their values or beliefs. Instead, we approach different perspectives with curiosity and empathy, seeking to understand the underlying motivations, experiences, and cultural influences that shape someone's values. Non-judgment does not mean that we abandon our own values or compromise our principles. It simply means that we strive to recognize the validity of diverse viewpoints, even if they differ from our own. It involves acknowledging that there are multiple paths to fulfillment, and each person's values are shaped by their unique life experiences, upbringing, and cultural background.

By practicing non-judgment, we create an environment that encourages open dialogue and fosters mutual respect. It allows for meaningful conversations and the exchange of ideas without the fear of being judged or dismissed. Through non-judgment, we can learn from others, broaden our perspectives, and deepen our understanding of the world.

Non-judgment also promotes compassion and empathy. It recognizes that we are all on our own individual journeys and that our values are deeply personal. By refraining from judgement, we can develop a genuine sense of empathy, appreciating the complexity of human experiences and the diverse range of values that exist.

In understanding our own core values, non-judgment plays a vital role. It allows us to explore our values with an open mind and without self-criticism. By embracing non-judgment, we create a safe space for self-reflection and self-discovery, enabling us to gain clarity about what truly matters to us and why.

2. INTEGRITY:

Integrity is another fundamental principle of value that shapes the way we live our lives and interact with others. It's about being true to ourselves and staying aligned with our core values, even when faced with challenges or temptations. When we embody integrity, we act in a way that is honest, ethical, and consistent with our beliefs.

Integrity means doing the right thing, even when no one is watching. It's about being accountable for our actions and taking responsibility for the impact they may have on ourselves and those around us. When we have integrity, we strive to make choices that are morally upright and fair, regardless of external influences or potential personal gain.

Imagine you're faced with a situation where you could easily cut corners or bend the rules to achieve a desired outcome. However, your commitment to integrity would guide you to take the higher road. You would choose to follow the path of honesty and transparency, even if it may be more challenging or require more effort. This is because you understand that integrity is not just about the end result, but also about the process and the values we uphold along the way.

Integrity also involves consistency. It means aligning our actions with our words and beliefs, ensuring that there is harmony between what we say and what we do. This consistency builds trust and credibility, as others can rely on us to act in accordance with our stated values. When we have integrity, we become people of our word, fostering strong relationships and a sense of reliability in our personal and professional lives. Integrity extends beyond our interactions with others; it also encompasses our relationship with ourselves. It involves being true to who we are and living in accordance with our own principles. It requires self-awareness and the willingness to reflect on our actions and intentions. By cultivating integrity, we can develop a sense of inner peace and self-respect, knowing that we are living in alignment with our authentic selves.

It's important to note that embodying integrity doesn't mean we are perfect or immune to mistakes. We are all human and can make errors in judgement. However, integrity means owning up to our mistakes, making amends when necessary, and learning from those experiences to grow and improve. So, integrity is about living with honesty, ethical conduct, and consistency. It's about staying true to our core values, even when faced with challenges or temptations. By embodying integrity, we create a strong foundation for building trustworthy relationships, personal growth, and a life of authenticity and fulfillment.

3. COMPASSION AND EMPATHY:

Compassion and empathy are two powerful qualities that enhance our ability to connect with and understand others. They allow us to navigate the complexities of human emotions and experiences with kindness, understanding, and a genuine desire to alleviate suffering. Compassion is the capacity to recognize and empathize with the pain, struggles, or challenges that others may be going through. It involves extending care, support, and understanding to others, even if we have not personally experienced exactly what they are going through. Compassion allows us to cultivate a sense of common humanity, acknowledging that we all face our own hardships and that no one is immune to suffering. Imagine a friend who is going through a difficult time. They might be dealing with a loss, a setback, or a personal challenge. Compassion would enable you to put yourself in their shoes, to truly understand and empathize with their feelings. It would move you to offer a listening ear, a comforting presence, or a helping hand, demonstrating your genuine concern and care. Empathy, on the other hand, is the ability to understand and share the emotions of others. It involves stepping into someone else's emotional experience, seeing the world through their eyes, and feeling what they might be feeling. Empathy is a key component of compassion because it helps us connect on a deeper level with others, fostering a sense of understanding and support. When we practice empathy, we actively listen to others without judgement, seeking to truly understand their perspective and emotions. We set aside our own biases and preconceptions, allowing ourselves to be fully present and receptive to their experiences. Through empathy, we validate the emotions of others, providing them with a safe space to express themselves and feel heard. Combining compassion and empathy allows us to extend kindness and understanding to others in a profound way. It helps us build bridges of connection, foster healthy relationships, and create a supportive and inclusive community. Compassion and empathy break down barriers, encourage communication, and promote mutual respect and understanding.

It's important to note that compassion and empathy are skills that can be developed and strengthened with practice. By cultivating a mindset of openness, curiosity, and genuine care for others, we can enhance our ability to empathize and respond compassionately to those around us.

Compassion and empathy are powerful qualities that enable us to connect with others on a deep emotional level. They allow us to extend kindness, understanding, and support, fostering a sense of community and creating meaningful relationships. By embracing compassion and empathy, we contribute to a more compassionate world where everyone feels seen, heard, and valued.

4. EVOLUTION AND REFLECTION:

Evolution and reflection are two essential processes that contribute to personal growth, self-awareness, and the development of a fulfilling life journey. They involve embracing change, learning from experiences, and continuously seeking improvement and self-discovery.

Evolution is the process of gradual development and transformation over time. It acknowledges that we are constantly evolving beings, shaped by our experiences, interactions, and the lessons we learn along the way. Just as the world around us evolves, we too have the capacity to evolve mentally, emotionally, and spiritually.

Imagine looking back on your life and reflecting on the person you were a few years ago. You might notice the growth and progress you've made, the new perspectives you've gained, and the lessons you've learned. Evolution means recognizing that we are not stagnant beings, but rather capable of embracing change and continuously expanding our knowledge, skills, and understanding of the world.

Reflection is the deliberate and introspective examination of our thoughts, actions, and experiences. It involves pausing, stepping back, and taking the time to contemplate and evaluate our choices, beliefs, and values. Reflection allows us to gain deeper insights into ourselves, our motivations, and the impact of our actions on ourselves and others.

Through reflection, we can identify patterns, strengths, and areas for growth. It enables us to recognize recurring themes in our lives, understand our reactions to certain situations, and make conscious adjustments to align our behavior with our values. Reflection helps us become more self-aware, enhancing our ability to make intentional choices and lead a more authentic and fulfilling life.

Both evolution and reflection are interconnected. By engaging in reflection, we gain valuable insights that inform our personal evolution. Reflection helps us identify areas where we can grow, develop new skills, or challenge our limiting beliefs. It encourages us to embrace change, explore new possibilities, and adapt to the ever-changing circumstances of life. Through this process, we become active participants in our own personal growth and transformation. We learn from our experiences, integrate new knowledge and perspectives, and continually evolve into more compassionate, wise, and resilient individuals.

It's important to note that evolution and reflection are ongoing processes. They require a willingness to embrace change, a commitment to self-exploration, and a genuine curiosity about our own potential. By actively engaging in reflection and being open to growth, we can navigate life's challenges with greater resilience, deepen our self-understanding, and shape a life that aligns with our authentic selves.

5. CONSISTENCY:

Consistency is a quality that encompasses reliability, steadfastness, and the ability to maintain a certain level of behavior or performance over time. It involves acting in alignment with our values, principles, and commitments consistently, regardless of external circumstances or pressures.

When we practice consistency, we strive to match our words with our actions. Imagine a situation where you have made a promise to someone. Consistency means following through on that promise, even when it requires effort or sacrifices on your part. It demonstrates trustworthiness and reliability, showing that others can rely on you to deliver on your commitments.

Consistency also involves maintaining a steady and stable approach in various areas of our lives. Whether it's our work, relationships, or personal goals, consistency allows us to build momentum, progress, and achieve long-term success. It means showing up consistently, putting in the necessary effort, and staying committed to our objectives.

By practicing consistency, we establish a foundation of trust and credibility in our interactions with others. People can rely on us to act predictably and follow through on our words, strengthening the bonds of trust and fostering healthier relationships. Consistency also contributes to building a positive reputation and a sense of dependability, both personally and professionally.

Consistency is not about perfection or inflexibility. It acknowledges that setbacks and obstacles are part of life. However, even in the face of challenges, consistency means maintaining our focus, resilience, and commitment to our values and goals. It involves learning from failures and adapting our approach, while still staying true to our core principles.

Consistency also plays a crucial role in personal growth and development. When we consistently engage in practices that align with our values and aspirations, we create habits that lead to positive change. Consistency allows us to reinforce desired behaviors, learn from mistakes, and make progress towards our personal and professional goals.

However, it's important to strike a balance with flexibility. While consistency is valuable, there may be times when adjustments or adaptations are necessary. Being consistent does not mean being rigid or resistant to change. It means having a clear understanding of our values and goals while remaining open to new insights and adapting our approach when appropriate.

Two questions you should ask yourself about consistency when approaching something significant in your daily life are:

1. How can I ensure consistency in living my core values across different areas of my life?
2. What are some strategies I can employ to stay consistent in my actions and behaviors aligned with my values?

By answering these questions on a written note will enhance your chances for a better life. Always write down your ideas to serve as a reminder of your plans.

Understanding your core values is not just a theoretical exercise but a practical tool that can profoundly impact your life. It is through this understanding that you gain clarity about who you are, what you believe in, and how you want to live your life. By identifying and aligning with your core values, you establish a strong foundation for making decisions, pursuing goals, and nurturing relationships that are in harmony with your authentic self. Your core values serve as a compass, guiding you through the complexities of life and helping you navigate the various choices and challenges that come your way. They provide a sense of direction, purpose, and motivation, allowing you to tap into your inner reservoirs of passion and drive. With your values as your guiding light, you can make choices with confidence, knowing that they align with your deepest beliefs and principles. Understanding your core values also empowers you to set healthy boundaries and make choices that prioritize your well-being and happiness. By knowing what truly matters to you, you can assertively protect your values and avoid compromising situations or relationships that may undermine your sense of self. This self-awareness allows you to cultivate a strong and authentic sense of identity, contributing to your overall growth and fulfillment. Moreover, understanding your core values enables you to make intentional use of your time and energy. By aligning your actions and priorities with your values, you can focus on what truly matters, avoiding distractions and unnecessary commitments that drain your resources. This focused approach allows you to live a more balanced and fulfilling life, where your time and energy are directed towards the things that bring you joy, fulfillment, and personal growth. In essence, understanding your core values is a journey of self-discovery, introspection, and reflection. It requires you to delve deep into your beliefs, explore your passions, and clarify your priorities. By embarking on this journey, you open yourself up to a life that is grounded in authenticity, purpose, and fulfillment. So, take the time to explore your core values, examine what truly matters to you, and let them serve as your guiding principles. Embrace your values as an integral part of your identity and allow them to shape your actions, decisions, and relationships. By doing so, you can live a life that is true to yourself and experience a profound sense of meaning, fulfillment, and alignment in all that you do.

III. Reflecting on Your Life's Journey

Bill was known for his insatiable curiosity and unwavering determination. He had a vision to revolutionize the world of technology. Driven by his passion, Bill and his friend Paul Allen started a small company called Microsoft in a tiny garage. With their relentless pursuit of innovation, they created groundbreaking software that would change the way people interacted with computers forever. As years went by, Microsoft grew from a small startup to a global powerhouse, and Bill Gates became a household name. Yet, he never lost sight of his mission to make technology accessible to all. Through the Bill & Melinda Gates Foundation, he dedicated his wealth and knowledge to improving education, eradicating diseases, and empowering people around the world. Bill's story is a testament to the power of dreams and the impact one person can have on the world. From a humble beginning to a philanthropic giant, he showed that with passion, perseverance, and a desire to make a difference, even the loftiest aspirations can become reality. And so, Bill Gates continues to inspire generations, reminding us that the power to change the world lies within our hands, waiting to be unleashed through unwavering dedication and a commitment to creating a better tomorrow.

As we navigate through the twists and turns of life, it's only natural to take a moment to pause and reflect on the path we have travelled. Our life's journey is a tapestry of experiences, emotions, and lessons that shape who we are and who we will become. It is a collection of memories, achievements, and challenges that have moulded us into the individuals we are today. So, let us embark on a journey of introspection, as we delve into the significance of reflecting on our life's journey. When we reflect on our life's journey, we gain a deeper understanding of ourselves. We uncover the layers that make us unique, discovering our strengths, weaknesses, and values. Through introspection, we become more self-aware, recognizing the patterns that have influenced our decisions and actions. By understanding ourselves better, we can make informed choices and align our lives with our true aspirations and dreams.

Moreover, reflecting on our life's journey allows us to appreciate the experiences we have had. Life is a collection of moments, both big and small, and by revisiting those moments, we can relive the joy, the pain, and the growth they brought us. We cherish the relationships we have cultivated, the milestones we have achieved, and the challenges we have overcome. Each experience has contributed to our personal growth, shaping us into resilient, compassionate, and wise individuals. In the process of reflection, we also gain a broader perspective. Life's challenges, setbacks, and failures can feel overwhelming in the moment, but when we step back and examine the bigger picture, we realize their role in our development. The trials we faced have taught us valuable lessons and given us the opportunity to build resilience and perseverance. By acknowledging both the highs and lows of our journey, we gain wisdom and find meaning in the face of adversity.

Furthermore, reflecting on our life's journey helps us set new goals and intentions for the future. As we contemplate the path we have travelled, we can assess whether we are living in alignment with our authentic selves. Are we pursuing our passions? Are we fostering meaningful relationships? Are we making a positive impact on the world around us? By evaluating our past choices and experiences, we can course-correct and set new intentions that align with our values and aspirations. In the hustle and bustle of everyday life, it's easy to get caught up in the relentless pursuit of success and forget to pause and reflect.

However, taking the time to reflect is essential for personal growth and fulfillment. It allows us to reconnect with our true selves, evaluate our progress, and realign our actions with our values.

To embark on this introspective journey, find a quiet space where you can be alone with your thoughts. Set aside distractions and let your mind wander through the memories and experiences that have shaped you. Write in a journal, meditate, or simply sit in silence. As you reflect, ask yourself thought-provoking questions such as:

- What are the defining moments in my life and how have they influenced me?
- What are my core values and am I living in alignment with them?
- What lessons have I learned from my successes and failures?
- Are there any changes I need to make to create a more fulfilling future?
- How have my relationships impacted my personal growth?

Remember, reflecting on your life's journey is not about dwelling on regrets or missed opportunities. It is about acknowledging the past, embracing the present, and envisioning a future that aligns with your deepest desires. Our conscious mind represents our awareness of the present moment, while our subconscious mind holds the vast reservoir of our memories, emotions, and beliefs. By understanding how these two aspects of our mind interact, we can gain valuable insights into our life's journey. Our conscious mind is an active participant in our daily experiences. It is the part of our mind that is engaged in decision-making, problem-solving, and rational thinking. When we consciously reflect on our life's journey, we engage in introspection, examining our thoughts, emotions, and actions. We consciously recall past events, assess their impact on us, and make connections between different aspects of our life. This process allows us to gain clarity and a conscious understanding of our life's trajectory.

However, it is important to recognize that our subconscious mind plays a significant role in shaping our perceptions, beliefs, and behavior. It operates beneath the surface, outside our immediate awareness. Our subconscious mind is like a vast library, storing all the experiences, emotions, and memories we have accumulated throughout our life. It holds the key to our deep-seated beliefs, fears, desires, and patterns of behavior. When we reflect on our life's journey, we tap into the power of our subconscious mind. It is through this process that we can access hidden insights, buried emotions, and forgotten memories. The subconscious mind has a way of bringing forth relevant information and associations that our conscious mind may have overlooked. It may reveal underlying patterns, recurring themes, and the root causes of certain behaviors or reactions. The subconscious mind also influences our perception of the world around us. Our beliefs and attitudes, many of which are deeply ingrained in our subconscious, shape the lens through which we view our experiences. For example, if we hold limiting beliefs about ourselves, such as "I am not good enough" or "I don't deserve happiness," they will colour our interpretation of events and affect our self-esteem. By becoming aware of these subconscious beliefs, we can challenge and reframe them, opening up new possibilities for growth and transformation.

One powerful technique for accessing the wisdom of our subconscious mind is through practices such as meditation, visualization, and journaling. These techniques create a bridge between the conscious and subconscious realms, allowing us to tap into our intuition and inner guidance. They help quiet the chatter of our conscious mind and create space for insights and revelations to emerge. Incorporating the understanding of both the conscious and subconscious mind in our reflection on our life's journey can lead to profound self-discovery and personal growth. By actively engaging our conscious mind in introspection, we can bring awareness to our thoughts, emotions, and actions. Simultaneously, by tapping into our subconscious mind, we can uncover deeper layers of our being, revealing hidden beliefs, motivations, and patterns.

Remember, the process of reflecting on your life's journey is a dynamic and ongoing one. It is a journey of self-discovery and self-compassion. By consciously exploring your experiences and engaging with your subconscious mind, you can gain valuable insights, heal emotional wounds, and create a more authentic and fulfilling future. In conclusion, reflecting on your life's journey is a deeply personal and transformative process that holds immense value. It is an opportunity to pause, introspect, and make sense of the experiences and lessons that have shaped your path. Through self-reflection, you gain a deeper understanding of yourself, your values, and your purpose. It allows you to appreciate the triumphs and achievements, acknowledge the challenges and setbacks, and embrace the growth and transformation that have occurred along the way. Engaging in self-reflection encourages gratitude for the people, opportunities, and moments that have enriched your life. It helps you recognize the patterns, habits, and beliefs that may no longer serve you, enabling you to make intentional choices and positive changes. Self-reflection also allows you to identify your strengths and weaknesses, fostering personal growth and development. Moreover, reflecting on your life's journey helps you gain perspective. It allows you to see the bigger picture, connect the dots, and find meaning in the various chapters of your life. It provides clarity and direction, guiding you towards your aspirations and dreams. Through self-reflection, you can uncover your passions, values, and purpose, leading to a more fulfilling and authentic life. Additionally, self-reflection instils a sense of resilience and self-compassion. By acknowledging your past experiences and embracing both the successes and failures, you cultivate resilience, learning to adapt and bounce back from adversity. It also nurtures self-compassion, as you come to understand that mistakes and imperfections are an integral part of the human experience, offering valuable opportunities for growth and learning.

Ultimately, reflecting on your life's journey is a continuous process, one that evolves with you. It is a powerful tool for self-discovery, personal growth, and creating a life aligned with your values and aspirations. Embrace the lessons learned, celebrate your accomplishments, and keep moving forward with a renewed sense of purpose and authenticity. Your life's journey is a unique and beautiful story, and through reflection. As we move on to the next chapter you'll understand more on the power of unveiling your purpose.

CHAPTER THREE

<u>Embracing the Power of Intuition</u>

"Success is not determined by how many times you fall, but by how many times you rise."

In a world driven by logic and rationality, the power of intuition often gets overlooked. Yet, intuition is an innate gift that lies within each of us, waiting to be acknowledged and embraced. It is a profound sense of knowing that transcends conscious reasoning, allowing us to tap into a deeper well of wisdom and insight. When we learn to trust and cultivate our intuition, we unlock a powerful tool for decision-making, creativity, and personal growth. Intuition is often described as a gut feeling or a hunch—an inner knowing that arises without conscious thought. It bypasses the limitations of the analytical mind and taps into a vast reserve of information and experience that may not be readily accessible to our conscious awareness. It's like a compass, guiding us towards what feels right and aligns with our authentic selves.

One of the greatest benefits of embracing intuition is its role in decision-making. While the rational mind can be valuable in weighing pros and cons and considering logical factors, intuition adds an extra dimension to the process. Intuition can help us see beyond the surface-level information and uncover deeper truths. It can provide a sense of clarity and direction when faced with difficult choices, helping us make decisions that are in harmony with our values and aspirations. Intuition is not limited to major life decisions; it can also guide us in everyday situations. Have you ever had a strong feeling to take a different route home and later discovered that it avoided a traffic jam? Or perhaps you've met someone new and instantly felt a connection or a sense of unease. These are all instances where intuition is at play, offering valuable insights that can enhance our experiences and keep us safe. Embracing intuition also fuels creativity and innovation. The great inventors, artists, and visionaries throughout history often credit their intuitive insights as the source of their groundbreaking ideas. Intuition opens the door to unconventional thinking and novel approaches, as it taps into our subconscious and allows us to make connections that elude our conscious minds. By embracing intuition, we access a wellspring of inspiration and originality, enabling us to think beyond boundaries and create something truly unique.

Moreover, intuition can be a potent tool for personal growth and self-discovery. When we learn to listen to our inner voice, we gain deeper insights into our own desires, passions, and purpose. Intuition can help us navigate through challenges, overcome obstacles, and find meaning in our experiences. By embracing our intuition, we foster a stronger connection with ourselves and a greater sense of authenticity and fulfillment.

However, embracing intuition does not mean disregarding logic or ignoring critical thinking. Rather, it means finding a balance between the two. Intuition and reason can work hand in hand, complementing each other to provide a more holistic perspective. By integrating both, we create a synergy that allows us to make informed decisions while tapping into the deeper wisdom within us. To embrace the power of intuition, it is essential to cultivate practices that enhance our ability to listen and trust our inner voice. Meditation, mindfulness, and quiet reflection can help quiet the noise of the external world and attune us to our intuitive insights. Paying attention to our bodily sensations and emotions can also provide valuable cues from our intuition. Additionally, journaling and creative expression can serve as powerful channels for intuitive exploration.

Anthony Reynold embarked on a journey of self-discovery with an insatiable curiosity burning within him. From a young age, he had a deep yearning to explore the depths of his own being and uncover the truths that lay hidden within. As he ventured into the vast landscape of his inner world, Anthony discovered the power of intuition and embraced it as his guiding light. Throughout his journey, Anthony encountered numerous challenges that tested his resolve and pushed him to his limits. Yet, it was during these moments of adversity that his intuition proved to be his greatest ally. It whispered words of encouragement, guiding him towards the path of resilience and growth. With each hurdle he overcame, Anthony's trust in his intuition grew stronger, and he learned to rely on it as a constant companion. In his quest for self-discovery, Anthony delved into various spiritual practices, seeking wisdom and enlightenment. Meditation became a cornerstone of his daily routine, allowing him to quiet his mind and tap into the depths of his intuition. Through these moments of stillness, he found clarity and a profound connection to his inner voice.

As Anthony's intuition deepened, he began to notice the subtle whispers of his heart. It led him to explore creative outlets such as painting and writing, unleashing a torrent of self-expression. The canvas became his sanctuary, where he could translate the language of his intuition into vibrant strokes of colour and evocative imagery. Through his artistic endeavours, he discovered a newfound sense of freedom and authenticity. Anthony's journey of self-discovery also took him on a physical odyssey, traversing different landscapes and immersing himself in diverse cultures. He sought inspiration from nature's grandeur, finding solace and peace in the mountains, forests, and vast oceans. These encounters with the natural world served as a reminder of the interconnectedness of all things and the wisdom that resides within the Earth itself.

Along his path, Anthony encountered fellow travellers who shared his yearning for self-discovery. They formed a tribe of like-minded souls, supporting and uplifting each other on their respective journeys. Together, they embraced the power of intuition and created a sacred space for growth, reflection, and profound conversations. As Anthony continued to embrace his intuition, he witnessed a transformation unfolding within him. He shed layers of societal conditioning, releasing old beliefs and limitations that had once held him back. With each step forward, he reclaimed his true essence, embracing his passions, strengths, and vulnerabilities with an unwavering authenticity. Through his journey, Anthony realized that intuition was not merely a tool but a way of life—a way of being fully present and attuned to the subtle whispers of the universe. It guided him to make choices that aligned with his deepest desires and values. It allowed him to navigate the complexities of life with grace and purpose, finding meaning in even the most challenging experiences. Anthony Reynold's journey of self-discovery continues to unfold, as he embraces the ever-evolving nature of his intuition. With each passing day, he grows more connected to his inner wisdom, expanding his capacity for love, compassion, and self-acceptance. He embodies the power of intuition, inspiring others to embark on their own transformative journeys and discover the infinite potential that resides within.

Certainly! Here are five crucial elements to remember when embracing the power of intuition; obtain a notepad and jot these ideas down; they will serve as a reminder in the days ahead:

1. **Seek solitude and silence**
2. **Embrace mistakes as learning opportunities**
3. **Practice discernment**
4. **Pay attention to your body's signals**
5. **Trust your gut**

Allow me to clarify the above key points to you; they will assist you in revealing your inner intuitions.

1. SEEK SOLITUDE AND SILENCE

Seeking solitude and silence refers to intentionally creating moments of stillness and quiet in your life. It involves finding time and space away from external distractions, allowing yourself to be alone with your thoughts and emotions. Solitude and silence provide a conducive environment for deep reflection, introspection, and a heightened connection with your intuition. In our fast-paced and technology-driven world, it's easy to be constantly bombarded by external stimuli such as notifications, social media, and the demands of daily life. This constant noise can cloud our thoughts and make it challenging to hear the subtle whispers of our intuition. Seeking solitude and silence is a deliberate act of stepping away from the external noise to create an inner sanctuary where we can reconnect with our inner selves. Solitude grants us the opportunity to disconnect from the external world and focus on our internal landscape. It allows us to tune in to our own thoughts, emotions, and desires without the influence or expectations of others. This intentional alone time provides space for self-reflection, introspection, and a deeper understanding of our own needs, values, and aspirations. It is in these moments of solitude that our intuition often becomes more pronounced and accessible. Silence, on the other hand, refers not only to the absence of external noise but also to cultivating a sense of inner stillness. It involves quieting the mental chatter and finding a sense of inner calm. By creating a peaceful environment free from distractions, we can tune in to the subtle messages of our intuition.

In the solitude and silence, our intuition has room to speak and be heard. It is in these tranquil moments that our inner voice becomes clearer, and intuitive insights can surface more easily. By giving ourselves the gift of solitude and silence, we create a sacred space for introspection, self-discovery, and a deepening of our intuitive connection. Practicing solitude and silence can take various forms depending on personal preferences. It could involve going for walks in nature, spending time in a quiet room or meditating, journaling, or engaging in activities that promote relaxation and introspection. The key is to intentionally carve out time for yourself, away from external distractions, to cultivate a sense of inner stillness and create an environment where your intuition can thrive.

2. EMBRACING MISTAKES AS LEARNING OPPORTUNITIES

Embracing mistakes as learning opportunities is an essential mindset to cultivate on your journey of personal growth and self-discovery. It involves shifting your perspective on mistakes from something to be avoided or ashamed of to valuable stepping stones on the path to success and wisdom. By embracing mistakes, you open yourself up to valuable lessons, growth, and a deeper understanding of yourself. You see, making mistakes is an inherent part of being human. We all stumble, falter, and make choices that don't turn out as we had hoped. But instead of dwelling on the negative aspects of mistakes, it is far more empowering to view them as opportunities for growth and learning. Mistakes provide valuable feedback and insights into what works and what doesn't. They shine a light on areas where we can improve, develop new skills, and gain a greater understanding of ourselves and the world around us.

When you embrace mistakes as learning opportunities, you adopt a mindset of curiosity and resilience. Rather than being discouraged or afraid of making mistakes, you approach them with a sense of openness and willingness to learn. You recognize that mistakes are not failures but stepping stones on the path to success. Each mistake brings you one step closer to achieving your goals and becoming the best version of yourself. Embracing mistakes as learning opportunities also frees you from the fear of judgement or perfectionism. It allows you to let go of unrealistic expectations and the pressure to always get things right. Instead, you recognize that mistakes are simply part of the journey, and they do not define your worth or potential. By embracing mistakes, you give yourself permission to take risks, explore new avenues, and step outside of your comfort zone.

Moreover, when you approach mistakes with a learning mindset, you become an active participant in your own growth and development. You take responsibility for your actions and choices, seeking to understand what went wrong and how you can improve. This self-reflection and self-awareness are key components of personal growth. By embracing mistakes, you gain valuable insights into your strengths, weaknesses, and areas for improvement. Remember, the most successful and accomplished individuals in any field have encountered their fair share of mistakes along the way. They have used these experiences as opportunities to learn, adapt, and refine their skills. By embracing mistakes, you align yourself with a mindset shared by great thinkers, innovators, and leaders throughout history.

3. PRACTICE DISCERNMENT

Practicing discernment is a powerful tool that allows you to navigate the complexities of life with clarity and wisdom. It involves developing the ability to distinguish between different choices, ideas, and perspectives, and making thoughtful judgments based on your values and principles. By practicing discernment, you become more intentional and deliberate in your decision-making, ensuring that your choices align with your authentic self. It allows you to sift through the noise and find the truth that resonates with you personally. Discernment empowers you to question, investigate, and evaluate the information and ideas presented to you, rather than accepting them at face value. Practicing discernment requires a combination of critical thinking, self-reflection, and an understanding of your own values and priorities. It involves taking the time to explore different perspectives, seeking reliable sources of information, and considering the potential consequences of your choices. Discernment is not about being judgmental or overly skeptical; rather, it is about approaching each situation with a balanced and thoughtful mindset.

One of the key aspects of practicing discernment is understanding that not everything you encounter is necessarily true or beneficial for you. By cultivating discernment, you develop the ability to differentiate between what aligns with your values, aspirations, and personal growth, and what may lead you astray or hinder your progress. Discernment empowers you to make choices that are in alignment with your authentic self, leading to greater fulfillment and satisfaction in life. Practicing discernment also allows you to navigate the vast array of options and opportunities that come your way. It helps you avoid being swayed by societal pressures or external influences that may not be in line with your own vision and purpose.

Discernment helps you make choices that are true to who you are and what you desire, rather than simply following the crowd or succumbing to external expectations. However, it is important to note that practicing discernment is not about being closed-minded or dismissing different perspectives outright. It is about approaching each situation with an open and inquisitive mind, while also staying true to your own values and principles. Discernment enables you to engage in meaningful conversations and consider alternative viewpoints, while still making choices that resonate with your own truth.

4. PAY ATTENTION TO YOUR BODY'S SIGNALS

When it comes to navigating life's choices and experiences, it is crucial to pay attention to the signals that your body sends you. Your body is an incredible source of wisdom and intuition, constantly providing valuable information that can guide you towards what is truly right for you. By tuning in and listening to your body's signals, you gain access to a deeper level of self-awareness and understanding. Think about those moments when you've had a "gut feeling" or a sense of unease in a particular situation. Your body might have reacted with a tightening in your chest, a pit in your stomach, or a sense of heaviness. These physical sensations are not random; they are your body's way of communicating with you. Paying attention to these signals can help you make choices that are in alignment with your well-being and intuition. Similarly, your body can also provide positive signals when you're on the right path. Perhaps you've experienced a sense of lightness, energy, or excitement in certain situations. Your body might feel relaxed, at ease, or uplifted. These sensations can serve as affirmations that you are moving in a direction that aligns with your values and desires.

To pay attention to your body's signals, it's important to cultivate a sense of body awareness. Take moments throughout your day to check in with your body. Notice any tension, discomfort, or ease that you might be experiencing. Observe how your body responds to different people, environments, or decisions. Trust that your body's signals are valuable and valid, even if they may not always align with your rational mind. Engaging in practices like meditation, mindfulness, or body scans can also help you deepen your connection with your body. These practices allow you to quiet the mind, focus your attention inward, and observe the sensations and messages that your body is sending you. Over time, you'll become more attuned to the subtle cues and signals, strengthening your ability to rely on your body as a trusted guide.

Remember, your body is an integral part of who you are, and it holds a wealth of wisdom and intuitive insight. By paying attention to its signals, you gain a powerful ally in navigating life's choices and experiences. Trust in the wisdom that your body offers and let it guide you towards decisions and paths that are in harmony with your authentic self.

5. TRUST YOUR GUT.

It's a powerful piece of advice that can serve as a guiding light on your journey through life. Your gut feeling, that intuitive sensation deep within you, holds valuable wisdom that shouldn't be ignored. When you trust your gut, you tap into a profound source of guidance that can lead you towards decisions, relationships, and experiences that align with your true self. You know those moments when something just feels right or wrong, even when you can't fully explain why? That's your gut speaking to you. It's a subtle whisper, a hunch, or a knowing that arises from within, bypassing the noise of logic and analysis. It's a primal instinct that has been with you since the dawn of humanity, guiding your ancestors through the challenges of survival. Trusting your gut is like accessing a deep well of wisdom that has been passed down through generations. But here's the thing: trusting your gut can be daunting. Society often emphasizes the need for concrete evidence, logical reasoning, and rationality. It's easy to doubt or dismiss that intuitive feeling as irrational or illogical. However, the truth is that your gut has a unique way of perceiving the world—a way that goes beyond conscious understanding. It takes into account not just the surface-level facts, but also the subtle nuances, the energy, and the unspoken truths of a situation. Trusting your gut requires a leap of faith—a willingness to let go of the need for certainty and embrace the unknown. It means learning to listen to that inner voice, even when it goes against conventional wisdom or external expectations. Trusting your gut is about acknowledging your own inner compass, your personal truth, and having the courage to follow it.

To cultivate trust in your gut, practice tuning in and paying attention to those intuitive nudges. Notice the physical sensations that arise when faced with decisions or encounters. Does your body feel light and expansive, or does it tense up and contract? Become aware of the subtle shifts in your emotions, the whispers of insight, and the quiet knowing that emerges. Trust that your gut is providing you with valuable information, even if you can't fully articulate or rationalize it at the moment.

Remember, trusting your gut doesn't mean you should disregard logic or critical thinking. It's about finding a balance between your intuition and your intellect. When you integrate both, you access a more holistic perspective—one that combines the wisdom of your gut with the analytical powers of your mind. As we come to the conclusion of the five elections on embracing the power of intuition, I encourage you to trust your gut. Embrace that innate wisdom within you and let it guide you towards a life that feels authentic, purposeful, and true to who you are. Trust in your gut instincts, and you'll embark on a path that is uniquely yours—one filled with opportunities, growth, and a deep sense of fulfillment.

In a world that often emphasizes the importance of logic and rationality, embracing the power of intuition brings about a refreshing and transformative shift in perspective. By acknowledging and valuing our innate intuitive abilities, we unlock a wellspring of wisdom, insight, and creativity. Intuition serves as a trusted guide, leading us towards decisions and choices that are in alignment with our authentic selves. It allows us to transcend surface-level information and tap into a deeper understanding of ourselves and the world around us. It is through intuition that we can make choices that resonate with our values, passions, and aspirations, ultimately leading to a more fulfilling and purposeful life. Moreover, embracing intuition opens the doors to endless possibilities for personal growth and self-discovery. By listening to our inner voice and heeding its messages, we gain deeper insights into our desires, fears, and potential. Intuition can help us navigate challenges, overcome obstacles, and uncover hidden strengths within ourselves. It becomes a powerful tool for transformation, as it empowers us to step into our authenticity and live a life that is true to who we are. Embracing intuition does not imply disregarding logic or critical thinking. Instead, it involves finding a harmonious balance between intuition and reason. By integrating both aspects, we can make well-informed decisions that consider both our intuitive insights and logical analysis, thereby harnessing the full potential of our cognitive abilities. To embrace the power of intuition, it is essential to cultivate practices that strengthen our connection with our inner selves. Engaging in mindfulness, meditation, and reflection allows us to quiet the noise of the external world and attune ourselves to our intuitive wisdom. By practicing self-awareness and paying attention to our emotions and bodily sensations, we can tap into the valuable guidance that intuition provides. In a fast-paced and complex world, embracing intuition offers us a compass to navigate the uncertainties and choices that come our way. It reminds us to trust our instincts, honour our inner knowing, and embark on a journey of self-exploration and growth. By embracing the power of intuition, we step into a realm of endless possibilities, where creativity, insight, and authenticity flourish. So let us embrace our intuitive gifts, and may they guide us towards a life filled with purpose, joy, and profound fulfillment.

I.   Tuning into Your Inner Voice

Have you ever had a moment when you felt a deep knowing, a sense of clarity that came from within? It's as if a voice inside you whispered the answers you were seeking. This inner voice, often referred to as intuition, can be a powerful guide in our lives, leading us toward our true purpose and authentic selves. In this article, we will explore the concept of tuning into your inner voice and how it can be a transformative tool for self-discovery. In the hustle and bustle of our modern lives, we are often bombarded with external stimuli, from the demands of work and relationships to the constant flood of information from technology. Amidst all this noise, it's easy to lose touch with our inner selves. Tuning into your inner voice is about intentionally creating space for self-reflection and deep listening, allowing your intuition to rise above the noise.

So, how can you start tuning into your inner voice? The first step is to cultivate a practice of mindfulness. Mindfulness involves being fully present in the moment, observing your thoughts and emotions without judgement. By practicing mindfulness, you create a mental space that allows your inner voice to be heard. This can be done through activities such as meditation, journaling, or simply taking quiet walks in nature. As you begin to quiet your mind, you may notice that your inner voice speaks to you in different ways. It could be a subtle feeling in your gut, a gentle tug in a certain direction, or even a vivid image or dream. Pay attention to these signals, as they often hold valuable insights about your true desires and aspirations. Trusting and following your intuition can lead to greater fulfillment and alignment with your authentic self.

Another important aspect of tuning into your inner voice is learning to distinguish it from the voices of fear, doubt, and external influences. Society often bombards us with expectations and societal norms, making it challenging to discern our own desires from what others want for us. Take the time to reflect on your values, passions, and dreams, and ask yourself if the choices you're making align with your inner voice. Trust that you have the wisdom within you to make decisions that are right for you. It's important to note that tuning into your inner voice is not about ignoring logic or dismissing external guidance. Instead, it's about integrating your intuition with rational thinking and external information. By combining these different sources of guidance, you can make more informed decisions that honour both your inner wisdom and practical considerations.

Practicing self-care is another crucial element of tuning into your inner voice. Nurturing your physical, emotional, and mental well-being creates a foundation for clarity and connection with your inner self. Make time for activities that bring you joy and help you relax. Prioritize self-reflection and introspection, allowing yourself to explore your thoughts and emotions without judgement. By taking care of yourself, you create the space for your inner voice to be heard. As you continue to tune into your inner voice, remember that it's a lifelong journey.

Your inner voice will evolve and change as you grow and experience new things. Be patient and compassionate with yourself along the way. Embrace the process of self-discovery, and trust that your inner voice will guide you toward a more fulfilling and authentic life.

Tuning into your inner voice is a deeply personal and introspective process. It requires creating a space for self-reflection and learning to trust your intuition. The four steps to help you tune into your inner voice are:

STEP ONE: CREATE QUIET AND STILLNESS

Creating quiet and stillness is an essential step in tuning into your inner voice. It's about finding a calm and peaceful environment where you can be alone with your thoughts and emotions. Imagine a moment when you retreat to a quiet room, away from the noise and distractions of the outside world. This space becomes a sanctuary for you to reconnect with yourself. In this space, you can find solace and a sense of calm. It could be a cozy corner in your home, a tranquil park, or any place where you feel comfortable and undisturbed. By intentionally seeking out these moments of quiet, you create a conducive environment for self-reflection and deep listening. When you enter this space, it's important to eliminate distractions that might disrupt your inner focus. Put away your electronic devices, turn off notifications, and let go of the constant chatter that fills your mind. Give yourself permission to disconnect from the external world, even if it's just for a few minutes each day.
As you settle into this quiet space, take a few deep breaths and consciously release any tension or stress you may be holding. Allow your body and mind to relax. Be present in the moment, letting go of worries about the past or future. This moment is all about being here, right now. In this stillness, you can begin to observe your thoughts, emotions, and sensations without judgement. It's a time to simply be with yourself, to listen attentively to the whispers of your inner voice. As thoughts arise, let them come and go like passing clouds. Notice any patterns, recurring themes, or emotions that surface. These are the clues that your inner voice might be trying to communicate with you.
Creating quiet and stillness is not about suppressing or avoiding thoughts and emotions. It's about creating a container for them to arise and be acknowledged. By giving yourself permission to be still, you open up the space for self-awareness and self-discovery.
This practice of quiet and stillness can take many forms. You might choose to meditate, finding a comfortable position and focusing your attention on your breath or a specific point of focus. Or perhaps you prefer to sit in nature, immersing yourself in the sounds of birds chirping, the rustle of leaves, or the gentle flow of a nearby stream. Even journaling or engaging in creative activities can create a sense of quiet and stillness as you connect with your inner thoughts and feelings. Remember, creating quiet and stillness is a gift you give yourself—a space to reconnect, recharge, and tune into your inner voice. It's an invitation to explore the depths of your being and listen to the wisdom that resides within you. So, find that quiet corner, close your eyes, take a deep breath, and embrace the tranquility that awaits you and this will lead you to find your purpose in life.

STEP TWO: FOLLOW YOUR CURIOSITY

Following your curiosity is like embarking on a thrilling adventure guided by your own interests and passions. It's about embracing the spark of curiosity that ignites within you and allowing it to lead you on a journey of exploration and self-discovery. Think of a time when you stumbled upon a fascinating topic or stumbled upon a new hobby that piqued your interest. Remember how your curiosity propelled you forward, urging you to learn more, ask questions, and delve deeper into the subject. Following your curiosity is about honouring that natural inclination and giving yourself permission to explore the things that captivate your mind and heart. Curiosity is often a sign that your inner voice is nudging you toward something meaningful. It's an invitation to uncover hidden talents, untapped passions, or unexplored paths that align with your authentic self. By following your curiosity, you open yourself up to new experiences, perspectives, and opportunities for growth.

Start by paying attention to the topics, activities, or ideas that genuinely intrigue you. What captures your attention and sparks a sense of wonder? It could be anything from art and science to history, music, or even a particular skill you've always wanted to learn. Allow yourself to be drawn to these areas of curiosity without judgement or preconceived notions. Once you've identified your curiosity, take steps to actively explore it. Dive into books, articles, or online resources that expand your knowledge and understanding. Seek out classes, workshops, or communities where you can engage with others who share your curiosity. Embrace a beginner's mindset, willing to learn, make mistakes, and grow along the way.

As you follow your curiosity, you might find that it leads you down unexpected paths. It may challenge your preconceptions or push you outside your comfort zone. Embrace these moments of discomfort as opportunities for personal and intellectual growth. Trust that your curiosity is guiding you toward experiences and opportunities that align with your authentic self.

Remember, following your curiosity is not about achieving a specific outcome or meeting external expectations. It's about nurturing your inner flame of wonder and exploring the depths of your own interests and passions. It's about honouring your unique journey and allowing yourself to be captivated by the mysteries and beauty of life. Follow the trails of wonder that it unveils before you. Embrace the joy of discovery, the thrill of learning, and the fulfillment that comes from pursuing what genuinely excites you. Trust in your inner voice and the wisdom it holds. With curiosity as your guide, you'll embark on a remarkable journey of self-exploration and personal growth.

STEP THREE: PATIENCE ACTIVE LISTENING

Practicing active listening is like giving someone your full presence and attention, making them feel seen, heard, and valued. It's a powerful way to connect with others and foster deeper understanding and empathy in your conversations and relationships. Imagine a time when you engaged in a conversation with someone who truly listened to you. They maintained eye contact, nodded their head in understanding, and responded thoughtfully to what you were saying. How did that make you feel? Active listening is about offering that same gift to others. To practice active listening, start by being fully present in the conversation. Put aside distractions such as your phone or other tasks. Give the person your undivided attention, signaling that you genuinely care about what they have to say.

Maintain eye contact to show that you are engaged and focused on them. Non-verbal cues such as nodding or leaning in slightly can also indicate that you are actively listening and interested in their words. These small gestures can make a significant impact and create a safe space for open communication.

Another crucial aspect of active listening is suspending judgement. Be open-minded and refrain from forming opinions or interrupting the person while they are speaking. Allow them to express themselves fully and share their perspective without feeling judged or rushed. Empathy plays a vital role in active listening. Try to understand the emotions and experiences underlying the person's words. Put yourself in their shoes and imagine how they might be feeling. Reflect their emotions back to them to show that you are genuinely trying to understand and empathize with their situation. A key technique in active listening is reflective or paraphrasing. This involves summarizing and restating what the person has said in your own words. It shows that you are actively processing their words and ensures that you have understood their message correctly. It also gives the person an opportunity to clarify any misunderstandings or add more context to their thoughts.

Additionally, ask open-ended questions to encourage the person to share more and delve deeper into their thoughts and feelings. This demonstrates your genuine interest and encourages a more meaningful and in-depth conversation. Remember, active listening is about valuing the speaker's perspective and creating a supportive environment for open communication. It's not about imposing your own opinions or trying to fix problems. The focus is on understanding, empathy, and building stronger connections. By practicing active listening, you can enhance your communication skills and cultivate more meaningful relationships. You'll develop a reputation as someone who truly listens and cares, fostering trust and rapport with those around you. So, the next time you engage in a conversation, make a conscious effort to practice active listening. Your presence and attentiveness will make a world of difference to the person you're speaking with.

STEP FOUR: ENGAGE IN SELF-REFLECTION

Engaging in self-reflection is like having a conversation with yourself, exploring your thoughts, emotions, and experiences to gain deeper insight into who you are and what matters to you. It's an opportunity to pause, step back, and look inward, like a mirror that reveals the layers of your being. Let me share a short, interesting story to illustrate the power of self-reflection:

Once upon a time, there was a young woman named Maya who felt lost and uncertain about her path in life. She had followed the expectations of others, pursuing a career that seemed practical but didn't truly ignite her passion. As the days passed, Maya grew increasingly disconnected from her authentic self. One day, as Maya was sitting in her favorite park, she noticed an old tree. Its branches swayed gracefully in the breeze, as if whispering secrets to the wind. Inspired by the tree's stillness and wisdom, Maya decided to engage in a moment of self-reflection.

She closed her eyes, took a deep breath, and asked herself, "What brings me joy? What truly matters to me?" As Maya sat in silence, memories and emotions floated to the surface. She realized that she had always been captivated by storytelling, but had never given it the attention it deserved. In that moment of self-reflection, Maya realized that she wanted to pursue a career in writing, to use her words to inspire and connect with others. She felt a surge of excitement and purpose as she embraced this newfound clarity about her true passion. From that day forward, Maya committed herself to self-reflection as a regular practice. She set aside time each week to journal, meditate, and reflect on her journey. Through self-reflection, she gained a deeper understanding of her strengths, values, and desires, which guided her in making choices aligned with her authentic self.

Self-reflection doesn't have to be limited to grand moments like Maya's. It can be as simple as taking a few minutes each day to pause, breathe, and ask yourself meaningful questions. What are you grateful for? What challenges have you overcome? What lessons have you learned? By exploring these questions, you invite self-awareness and growth into your life. Imagine sitting across from a close friend, sipping a warm cup of tea, and engaging in a meaningful conversation. Self-reflection is similar, but instead of talking to someone else, you direct your attention inward and become both the speaker and the listener. In the busyness of life, it's easy to get caught up in the whirlwind of external demands and lose touch with ourselves. Engaging in self-reflection is a way to reconnect, to carve out a space where you can explore your inner landscape without judgment or distraction.

To begin, find a quiet and comfortable space where you can be alone with your thoughts. It can be a cozy corner of your home, a serene park, or even a favorite spot in nature. Allow yourself to settle into this peaceful environment, free from distractions, and give yourself permission to focus solely on your own thoughts and emotions. As you engage in self-reflection, start by asking yourself open-ended questions that invite introspection. What are your dreams, aspirations, and values? How do your experiences shape your beliefs and perceptions? What emotions are you currently feeling, and what might be the underlying causes?

Listen to the whispers of your inner voice as you contemplate these questions. Be open to the thoughts and feelings that arise within you, even if they seem uncomfortable or challenging. Self-reflection is about embracing the totality of who you are, including the parts that may be difficult to face. Writing in a journal can be a powerful tool for self-reflection. As you pour your thoughts onto the pages, you create a tangible record of your inner journey. It allows you to track patterns, recognize growth, and gain clarity as you delve deeper into your thoughts and emotions.

Engaging in self-reflection is not about seeking perfection or finding immediate solutions. It's a process of self-discovery and self-acceptance, a way to cultivate self-awareness and nurture personal growth. It's about honouring your own experiences and finding meaning in the lessons they offer. By engaging in self-reflection, you develop a stronger understanding of yourself and your desires. You become more attuned to your needs and values, allowing you to make choices that align with your authentic self. Self-reflection empowers you to live a life that is true to who you are, bringing fulfillment and a deeper sense of purpose. Start right now to create a space for self-reflection, where you can explore the depths of your thoughts, emotions, and experiences. Embrace the process of self-discovery, and let the insights you gain guide you on your journey of personal growth and fulfillment.

In conclusion, tuning into your inner voice is about creating space for self-reflection, deep listening, and mindfulness. It's about recognizing and honouring the intuitive wisdom within you. By cultivating this practice, you can gain valuable insights about your true desires, make decisions aligned with your authentic self, and navigate life with greater clarity and fulfillment. So, take a moment, close your eyes, and listen to the whispers of your inner voice. What is it telling you?

II.   Cultivating Intuitive Decision-Making

Making decisions can be a daunting task. Whether you're faced with career choices, personal dilemmas, or even what to have for dinner, the array of options can leave you feeling overwhelmed. In such situations, cultivating intuitive decision-making can be a powerful tool to help navigate the complexity and uncertainty of life. So, let's explore the art of nurturing your inner guide, unleashing the power of intuition. Intuition, often referred to as a gut feeling or sixth sense, is that subtle but potent force within us that provides insights and guidance beyond rational analysis. It taps into our accumulated experiences, knowledge, and emotions, offering a unique perspective that complements logical thinking. When harnessed effectively, intuition can lead us to make choices that align with our value The first step in cultivating intuitive decision-making is to develop self-awareness. Understanding ourselves, our emotions, and our values is crucial to connecting with our intuitive voice. Take time to reflect on your past experiences and identify moments when you trusted your instincts. Recall the outcomes of those decisions and analyze what factors influenced your choices. Recognizing patterns and tendencies will allow you to become more attuned to your intuitive signals.

Next, creating space for stillness and silence is essential as we had already discussed it above. In our fast-paced and noisy world, finding moments of tranquility can be challenging but immensely rewarding. Engaging in mindfulness practices, such as meditation or deep breathing exercises, can quiet the mind and open the channels to intuitive insights. As the noise subsides, you will find that your inner guide becomes clearer and more accessible. Listening to your body is another fundamental aspect of nurturing intuition. Our bodies often carry wisdom that our minds may overlook. Pay attention to physical sensations, emotions, and subtle cues that arise when faced with decisions. Notice if a particular option brings a sense of lightness or heaviness, relaxation or tension. These bodily responses can provide valuable information to guide your choices.

Developing trust in your intuition is crucial. Doubt and skepticism can cloud your judgement and prevent you from fully embracing your inner guide. Remember that intuition is not infallible, but it is a valuable source of wisdom that can complement logical thinking. Start by making small decisions based on your intuition and observe the outcomes. As you witness the positive impact of following your inner voice, your confidence will grow, making it easier to rely on intuition for more significant choices. Surrounding yourself with supportive individuals who value intuition can also be beneficial. Seek out mentors, friends, or communities that encourage and celebrate intuitive decision-making. Sharing your experiences and learning from others can deepen your understanding and provide a supportive network as you continue to nurture your intuitive abilities.

Finally, be patient with yourself. Cultivating intuitive decision-making is a lifelong journey that requires practice and perseverance. There may be times when your intuition leads you astray, but view these instances as learning opportunities rather than failures. Embrace the process of self-discovery and trust that your inner guide will continue to grow stronger with time and experience.

In conclusion, cultivating intuitive decision-making is a journey of self-discovery and empowerment. By honing this innate ability, you tap into a wellspring of wisdom that resides within you. Embracing your intuition allows you to navigate the complexities of life with greater clarity and confidence. While rational analysis has its merits, intuition adds a layer of insight that goes beyond logical reasoning. It connects you to your core values, passions, and aspirations, helping you make decisions that align with your authentic self. It guides you towards choices that are in harmony with your true desires and purpose.

Remember, intuition is not infallible, and there may be times when it leads you down unexpected paths. But even in those moments, there is wisdom to be gained. Trust in the process and embrace the lessons along the way. With practice, your intuitive decision-making skills will strengthen, and you will become more adept at discerning the subtle signals and messages from within. Cultivating intuitive decision-making is not a one-time task but a lifelong practice. It requires patience, self-awareness, and an openness to listen to the whispers of your intuition. As you nurture this inner guide, it will become a reliable compass that supports you in making choices that align with your highest good. In the end, by cultivating intuitive decision-making, you empower yourself to live a life that is guided by your deepest wisdom and authentic desires. Embrace the power of your intuition, and may it illuminate your path towards fulfillment, joy, and the realization of your true potential.

CHAPTER FOUR

Cultivating Authenticity

"Don't be afraid to give up the good to go for the great." - John D. Rockefeller

Authenticity, the quality of being genuine and true to oneself, is an essential aspect of personal growth and fulfillment. In a world often filled with social pressures, external expectations, and the desire for acceptance, it can be challenging to stay true to who we really are. However, cultivating authenticity is a transformative journey that leads to a deeper understanding of yourself and the ability to live a more meaningful and fulfilling life. At its core, authenticity is about embracing and expressing your true self without fear or judgement. It involves aligning your thoughts, feelings, values, and actions in a way that reflects your innermost desires, passions, and beliefs. When you are authentic, you live in congruence with your core identity, allowing your unique strengths and talents to shine through.

To cultivate authenticity, you must first embark on a journey of self-discovery. This involves taking the time to reflect on your values, interests, and passions. What brings you joy? What are your deepest desires and aspirations? Understanding your true self requires introspection and self-awareness. It involves being honest with yourself and acknowledging both your strengths and areas for growth.

Authenticity also involves embracing vulnerability. It also means being willing to show your true self to others, even when it feels uncomfortable or risky. Vulnerability allows you to connect with others on a deeper level, fostering genuine relationships built on trust and mutual understanding. When you let go of the masks you wear to fit in or please others, you create space for true connection and acceptance.

Cultivating authenticity requires us to let go of the need for external validation. It means finding the courage to be ourselves, even when others may not understand or approve of our choices. Seeking approval from others can lead to a life filled with dissonance and regret, as we sacrifice our own desires and values to meet societal expectations. Authenticity calls for embracing your uniqueness and realizing that your worth is not defined by others' opinions. Furthermore, practicing self-compassion is vital on the journey to authenticity. We are all imperfect beings, and it's essential to acknowledge and accept our flaws and mistakes. Instead of harsh self-judgement, self-compassion allows you to approach yourself with kindness and understanding. It enables you to learn from your experiences and grow, rather than getting stuck in a cycle of self-doubt or shame.

Authenticity extends beyond our individual lives; it also influences how we show up in the world. When you embrace your authenticity, you have the power to inspire and influence others positively. By being genuine and true to yourself, you give permission for others to do the same. Your authenticity becomes a beacon of light, encouraging those around you to embrace their own uniqueness and live authentically.

The story of John Wilson is one of resilience, determination, and a relentless pursuit of his dreams. John was born into a modest family in a small town. From a young age, he had a deep passion for music. He would spend hours listening to his favorite artists, mesmerized by the melodies and lyrics that seemed to speak directly to his soul. As John grew older, his love for music only intensified. He taught himself to play the guitar and started writing his own songs. He would spend countless nights in his room, strumming away, pouring his heart and emotions into his music. But his dreams went beyond his bedroom walls; he longed to share his songs with the world. However, John faced many obstacles along his journey. His family didn't understand his passion for music and urged him to pursue a more stable career. Despite their concerns, John couldn't ignore the fire burning within him. He knew that music was his calling, and he was determined to make it his life's work. Undeterred by the challenges, John started performing at local coffee shops and open mic nights. He poured his heart and soul into each performance, captivating audiences with his raw talent and genuine authenticity. His soulful voice and heartfelt lyrics resonated with people, and slowly but steadily, he began to build a small following.

But John's journey wasn't without setbacks. He faced numerous rejections from record labels and faced doubts from those around him. Many people told him that the music industry was a tough and unforgiving place, and success was reserved for the lucky few. Yet, John refused to let discouragement extinguish his dreams. Instead, he turned to the power of the internet. John started sharing his music on social media platforms, connecting with fans from around the world. He used his online presence to build a community of supporters who believed in his talent and authenticity. Through perseverance and a strong online presence, John's fan base grew, and his music started reaching a wider audience. One fateful day, a talent scout stumbled upon one of John's videos online. Captivated by his voice and songwriting skills, the talent scout reached out to John, offering him a chance to audition for a major record label. It was a dream come true for John, and he gave it his all during the audition, pouring his heart into each note. To his amazement, the record label recognized John's undeniable talent and signed him to a recording contract. It was the breakthrough he had been working tirelessly for, a validation of his unwavering dedication and belief in his craft.

With the support of his record label, John released his debut album, filled with songs that captured the essence of his journey, the highs and lows, and his unwavering authenticity. The album struck a chord with listeners worldwide, resonating with those who craved genuine and heartfelt music. John's success continued to soar as he embarked on a tour, performing his music to sold-out venues around the globe. But amidst the fame and recognition, John stayed grounded, always staying true to himself and the music he loved. He remained grateful to his fans and never lost sight of the passion that had propelled him forward.

John Wilson's story is a testament to the power of authenticity and perseverance. It serves as a reminder that no dream is too big or too distant if we remain true to ourselves and never give up on what truly sets our souls on fire. Through his music, John touched the lives of many, inspiring them to embrace their own authenticity and chase their dreams with unwavering determination.

The power of cultivating authenticity is profound and far-reaching. When you embrace and nurture your true self, you unlock a multitude of benefits that positively impact various aspects of your lives. There are six powerful effects of cultivating authenticity:

1. SELF-ACCEPTANCE:

Self-acceptance is a powerful practice that involves embracing and loving ourselves fully, just as we are, without judgement or conditions. It is an essential component of cultivating authenticity and living a fulfilling life. Let's explore the concept of self-acceptance together. Often, you are your own harshest critics. You set high expectations for yourself, compare yourself to others, and constantly find flaws within yourself. But self-acceptance invites you to let go of this self-judgement and embrace your entire being with kindness and compassion. To practice self-acceptance, you start by acknowledging and honouring your unique qualities, both positive and negative. It means recognizing your strengths, talents, and accomplishments, celebrating the aspects of yourself that you appreciate. But it also means acknowledging your imperfections, insecurities, and mistakes without shame or self-condemnation.

Self-acceptance is not about seeking perfection or denying areas where you want to grow and improve. Instead, it's about embracing your whole self, understanding that you are a human being with a range of experiences, emotions, and traits. It's about recognizing that your worthiness as an individual is not contingent on external validation or meeting societal standards.

When you practice self-acceptance, you free yourself from the burden of constantly striving for approval or trying to fit into moulds that don't align with your true self. You let go of the need to be someone else or to live up to the expectations imposed upon you by others. You grant yourself permission to be authentic, embracing your quirks, unique perspectives, and individual journeys.

Also self-acceptance is a transformative process that requires patience, self-compassion, and gentle self-reflection. It involves treating yourself with the same kindness and understanding that you would extend to a dear friend. It means being forgiving of your mistakes, failures, and setbacks, recognizing that they are essential parts of your growth and learning.

When you practice self-acceptance, you cultivate a deep sense of self-worth and inner peace. You learn to trust yourself, our instincts, and your abilities. You become more resilient in the face of challenges, knowing that you are inherently deserving of love, compassion, and happiness.

Furthermore, self-acceptance positively impacts our relationships with others. When we accept ourselves fully, we radiate an authentic energy that attracts and nurtures genuine connections. We can engage with others more openly and authentically, without the fear of judgement or the need to hide our true selves. Remember, you are deserving of love and acceptance exactly as you are. Embrace your strengths, accept your flaws, and honour your journey. Embracing self-acceptance allows you to shine authentically and live a life that aligns with your truest self.

2. ENHANCED RELATIONSHIP:

Enhanced relationships are a beautiful outcome of cultivating authenticity and embracing our true selves. When you prioritize authenticity in your connections with others, you've created a space for deep and meaningful relationships to flourish. Enhanced relationships are built on acceptance and understanding. When you accept yourself fully, flaws and all, you extend that same acceptance to others. You appreciate and celebrate their uniqueness, allowing them to feel seen, heard, and valued for who they truly are. This creates a safe and nurturing environment where relationships can thrive.

By being authentic, we encourage others to drop their masks and pretences, inviting them to show up authentically as well. This creates a beautiful synergy where both individuals feel comfortable being their genuine selves, free from the pressure to conform or please others. As a result, conversations become more honest, emotions are expressed more openly, and deeper connections are formed. Enhanced relationships are characterized by mutual respect and trust. When we embrace our authenticity, we communicate our boundaries, needs, and desires with clarity and honesty. We invite others to do the same, fostering a relationship dynamic based on open communication and mutual understanding. Trust is built through this genuine exchange, forming a solid foundation for deeper connections.

In enhanced relationships, there is a deep sense of connection and belonging. When we embrace our authenticity, we attract people who align with our true values and interests. These connections feel natural and effortless, as there is an inherent resonance between our authentic selves and theirs. We form bonds that are rooted in shared experiences, genuine appreciation, and mutual growth. Furthermore, enhanced relationships encourage personal growth. When we surround ourselves with authentic individuals who support and uplift us, we are inspired to grow and evolve. These relationships provide a nurturing environment where we can explore our potential, learn from one another, and challenge ourselves to become the best versions of ourselves. It's important to note that enhanced relationships require effort and investment from both sides. Authenticity is a two-way street, and both individuals must be willing to show up as their true selves and embrace vulnerability. By doing so, we create a powerful synergy that elevates the relationship to new heights.

3. INCREASED EMOTIONAL RESILIENCE:

Increased emotional resilience is a remarkable outcome of cultivating authenticity and embracing our true selves. It equips us with the ability to navigate life's challenges with strength and grace, allowing us to bounce back from setbacks and thrive in the face of adversity. Let's delve into the concept of increased emotional resilience together. Life is filled with ups and downs, and emotional resilience is our capacity to adapt, recover, and maintain a sense of inner balance amidst the various trials we encounter. When we cultivate authenticity, we develop a deep understanding and acceptance of our emotions. We acknowledge that experiencing a range of emotions is a natural part of the human experience, and we allow ourselves to fully feel and process them without judgement or suppression. By embracing our authentic selves, we develop a greater sense of self-awareness. We become attuned to our emotional needs and can effectively recognize and express our feelings. This self-awareness empowers us to navigate life's challenges with a heightened understanding of ourselves, enabling us to make choices and take actions that support our emotional well-being.

When we embrace authenticity, we also cultivate self-compassion. We treat ourselves with kindness and understanding, acknowledging that we are imperfect beings who are allowed to make mistakes and experience setbacks. Self-compassion allows us to extend forgiveness and grace to ourselves during difficult times, nurturing a resilient mindset that encourages growth and learning. Authenticity empowers us to tap into our inner strengths and resources. By embracing our true selves, we recognize and leverage our unique qualities and talents, which can contribute to increased emotional resilience. We draw upon our authentic values, interests, and passions to find meaning and purpose, serving as guiding lights during challenging moments. Additionally, embracing authenticity enables us to build a support network of genuine connections. When we show up as our true selves, we attract individuals who appreciate and value us for who we are. These authentic relationships provide a strong support system during difficult times, offering comfort, empathy, and guidance. The presence of a supportive community bolsters our emotional resilience, reminding us that we are not alone in our struggles. Cultivating authenticity allows us to reframe our perspective on challenges and setbacks. Instead of viewing them as insurmountable obstacles, we approach them with a growth mindset. We recognize that setbacks are opportunities for growth and learning, and we embrace them as valuable experiences that shape us into stronger and more resilient individuals. As we navigate life's inevitable storms with increased emotional resilience, we develop an unwavering belief in our ability to overcome adversity. We become more adaptable and flexible in the face of change, and we develop a greater sense of inner stability and confidence. With each challenge we conquer, our emotional resilience expands, preparing us to face future obstacles with courage and resilience.

4. CREATE EXPRESSION:

Creative expression is a beautiful and powerful means of communicating, connecting, and exploring the depths of our inner selves. It is a way to give voice to our thoughts, emotions, and unique perspectives. As human beings, we possess an innate desire to express ourselves creatively. It is an integral part of our being, allowing us to tap into our imagination, intuition, and personal experiences. Creative expression takes various forms such as art, music, writing, dance, photography, and more. It provides a means to communicate and share our inner world with others.

When we engage in creative expression, we access a realm of freedom and authenticity. It is a space where we can let go of inhibitions and societal expectations, embracing our true selves without judgement. In this state, we can fully explore and express our thoughts, feelings, and ideas in a way that is uniquely our own. Creative expression offers a sanctuary for self-discovery and self-reflection. Through various artistic mediums, we delve into the depths of our emotions, desires, and beliefs. It allows us to process and make sense of our experiences, offering a form of catharsis and healing. We give voice to our joys, sorrows, hopes, and fears, finding solace and understanding in the act of creation. Moreover, creative expression serves as a powerful means of communication. Sometimes, our deepest emotions and thoughts are challenging to express through conventional means. However, through creative outlets, we can convey complex ideas and sentiments that surpass the limitations of words. It allows us to connect with others on a profound level, evoking emotions, sparking conversations, and fostering empathy and understanding. When we engage in creative expression, we tap into our innate ability to innovate and bring something new into the world. It is an act of bringing our unique perspectives and ideas into tangible form. Through our creations, we offer a piece of ourselves to the world, contributing to the collective tapestry of human expression. Creative expression encourages us to embrace experimentation and risk-taking. It invites us to step outside our comfort zones, explore new techniques, and challenge ourselves to grow. In the process, we discover new facets of our creativity and unlock untapped potential, expanding the boundaries of our artistic capabilities.

Engaging in creative expression nurtures a sense of fulfillment and purpose. It provides a channel for our passions and interests, giving us a deep sense of satisfaction and joy. Whether it is through painting, writing, dancing, or any other creative pursuit, we experience a profound connection to our authentic selves and a sense of alignment with our true passions.

In summary, creative expression is a powerful form of self-discovery, communication, and personal growth. It allows us to embrace our authenticity, share our inner world, and connect with others on a deep level. Through creative expression, we find solace, meaning, and a means to explore the vast depths of our imagination and emotions. So, let your creativity flow, embrace your unique voice, and allow your authentic self to shine through your artistic expressions.

5. PERSONAL EMPOWERMENT:

Personal empowerment is a transformative state of being that allows you to take ownership of your life, make conscious choices, and cultivate a sense of inner strength and confidence. It is about recognizing and embracing your own power to create the life you desire. At its core, personal empowerment is about realizing that you have control over your thoughts, actions, and decisions. It is about shifting from a mindset of victimhood or helplessness to one of personal responsibility and agency. When you empower yourself, you understand that you have the ability to shape your own reality and create positive change. Personal empowerment begins with self-awareness. Take the time to reflect on your values, strengths, and passions. Understand what truly matters to you and what brings you joy and fulfillment. Self-awareness allows you to align your actions and choices with your authentic self, enabling you to live a life that is true to who you are. Embracing personal empowerment also means cultivating self-belief and self-confidence. Recognize your own worth and inherent capabilities. Celebrate your achievements, no matter how big or small, and acknowledge your unique talents and strengths. Embrace self-compassion and kindness, treating yourself with the same respect and support you would offer to a dear friend.

Personal empowerment is about setting clear goals and taking inspired action to achieve them. Define what success means to you and create a roadmap to reach your aspirations. Break down your goals into manageable steps, and take consistent action towards their realization. Remember that setbacks and challenges are part of the journey, but with determination and resilience, you have the power to overcome them. Taking responsibility for your own happiness and well-being is a vital aspect of personal empowerment. Recognize that your happiness is not dependent on external circumstances or the opinions of others. Instead, it comes from within. Focus on self-care, nourishing your mind, body, and spirit. Prioritize activities that bring you joy, practice mindfulness, and surround yourself with positive influences that uplift and inspire you.

Personal empowerment also involves setting and enforcing boundaries. Understand your limits and communicate them effectively. Learn to say no when something doesn't align with your values or priorities. Boundaries protect your energy, preserve your self-worth, and ensure that your time and resources are invested in what truly matters to you. Moreover, personal empowerment thrives in a supportive community. Surround yourself with like-minded individuals who uplift and encourage you. Seek out mentors and role models who inspire you to reach new heights. Engage in meaningful connections and collaborations that foster growth and mutual support.

By embracing personal empowerment, you tap into your inner reservoirs of strength, resilience, and creativity. You become the author of your own story, embracing your authentic self and living a life that aligns with your values and aspirations. Personal empowerment empowers you to embrace opportunities, overcome challenges, and live a life of purpose and fulfillment. Remember, personal empowerment is not a destination but a continuous journey. It requires self-reflection, self-belief, and a commitment to growth. Embrace your power, trust in your abilities, and let personal empowerment guide you towards a life of authenticity, joy, and personal fulfillment.

6. PERSONAL GROWTH AND FULFILLMENT:

Personal growth and fulfillment are intertwined aspects of our human journey. They encompass the process of continuous self-improvement, self-discovery, and embracing our true potential. Personal growth is the ongoing pursuit of expanding our knowledge, skills, and understanding of ourselves and the world around us. It involves seeking new experiences, challenging our beliefs, and embracing opportunities for learning and development. Through personal growth, we continuously evolve, broaden our perspectives, and deepen our self-awareness. When we embark on a path of personal growth, we open ourselves to new possibilities and embrace change. We step out of our comfort zones, take risks, and explore uncharted territories. Personal growth pushes us beyond our limits, encouraging us to overcome fears and embrace challenges that foster our growth. As we engage in personal growth, we develop a deeper understanding of our values, passions, and purpose. We align our actions and choices with our authentic selves, living in congruence with our core beliefs. This alignment brings a sense of fulfillment and meaning to your life, as you live in accordance with what truly matters to you.

Personal growth is not limited to acquiring external achievements or material success. It is a holistic journey that encompasses emotional, mental, and spiritual growth. It involves cultivating emotional intelligence, developing resilience, nurturing healthy relationships, and finding inner peace. It requires self-reflection, self-compassion, and the willingness to confront our fears and limitations.

Fulfillment is the deep sense of satisfaction and contentment that arises when we live in alignment with our authentic selves and purpose. It is not a destination but rather an ongoing state of being. When we experience fulfillment, we feel a profound sense of joy and peace that comes from living a life that is true to who we are. Fulfillment is unique to each individual and arises from embracing our passions, pursuing our dreams, and making a positive impact in the world. It is about finding purpose in our work, relationships, and contributions to society. When we align our actions with our values and use our strengths to serve others, we experience a deep sense of fulfillment and find a profound meaning in our existence.

Personal growth and fulfillment are interconnected. As we engage in personal growth, we expand our capacity for fulfillment, and as we experience fulfillment, we are motivated to continue growing. They create a positive feedback loop, fueling our desire to become the best versions of ourselves and live a life that aligns with our true purpose. Embracing personal growth and seeking fulfillment requires courage, self-reflection, and a willingness to embrace change. It involves stepping outside of our comfort zones, embracing challenges, and continuously learning and evolving. It is a lifelong journey that unfolds with each new experience and self-discovery.

In conclusion, cultivating authenticity is not a destination but an ongoing process that requires continuous self-reflection and growth. It is a commitment to living a life that is true to our core values, passions, and aspirations. By embracing authenticity, we unlock a sense of liberation and empowerment, allowing us to live with integrity and purpose. As we navigate the complexities of life, authenticity becomes a compass that guides our choices and decisions. It empowers us to make choices that align with our true selves, even when they may be difficult or unpopular. It encourages us to step outside our comfort zones, take risks, and embrace the fullness of our potential. Authenticity is a gift we give ourselves and the world around us. When we live authentically, we contribute to a more genuine and compassionate society. Our authentic presence becomes an invitation for others to be themselves, fostering an environment of acceptance and understanding.

I. Embracing Your True Self

Today, I want to talk to you about the transformative power of embracing your true self. In a world that often pressures us to conform, it is crucial to recognize the importance of authenticity and to nurture the unique qualities that make us who we are. Embracing your true self is a journey of self-discovery, self-acceptance, and self-love, and it is a path that can lead to personal fulfillment and genuine happiness. Authenticity begins with self-awareness. Take a moment to reflect on who you are at your core. What are your passions, dreams, and values? What makes your heart sing and your spirit soar? Embracing your true self means acknowledging these aspects of your identity and living in alignment with them. When you tap into your authentic self, you allow your true essence to shine through, creating a powerful and magnetic presence.

However, embracing your true self is not always easy. Society often imposes expectations and moulds us to fit predefined roles. We may find ourselves conforming to societal norms, suppressing our true thoughts and emotions, and living inauthentic lives. But deep down, we yearn to break free from these constraints and embrace our uniqueness. To embrace your true self, you must embark on a journey of self-acceptance. This requires embracing both your strengths and weaknesses, embracing your past mistakes and imperfections, and embracing the totality of your being. Remember that we are all beautifully flawed and that our imperfections make us human. Embrace them as opportunities for growth and learning, and celebrate the uniqueness they bring to your character. Self-love is another essential aspect of embracing your true self. Treat yourself with kindness, compassion, and respect. Cultivate a positive self-image and believe in your abilities. Practice self-care and prioritize activities that bring you joy and fulfillment. By nurturing a loving relationship with yourself, you develop the confidence and courage needed to embrace your true self and pursue your passions unapologetically.

Embracing your true self requires the courage to live authentically. It means standing up for your beliefs, even if they differ from the mainstream. It means speaking your truth, even when your voice trembles. Remember that you are not defined by the opinions of others. The opinions of society do not determine your worth. Your worth lies in being true to yourself and living in accordance with your values. When you embrace your true self, you inspire others to do the same. By living authentically, you create a ripple effect that encourages those around you to embrace their uniqueness as well. Your genuine expression of self becomes a beacon of hope and inspiration, reminding others that they too can be free from the chains of conformity. Embracing your true self also opens the doors to a fulfilling life. When you live authentically, you attract people and opportunities that align with your true desires. Authenticity breeds genuine connections, as others are drawn to your authentic energy and sincerity. By embracing who you truly are, you create a life that is in harmony with your deepest values and aspirations.

Let me explore to you the numerous benefits that come from embracing your true self. When you wholeheartedly accept and celebrate who you are, incredible transformations occur in various aspects of your life. Embracing your true self is not only empowering, but it also leads to personal growth, fulfillment, and an authentic sense of happiness. Let's dive into the remarkable benefits that await you on this journey of self-discovery.

1. **Authenticity and Inner Peace:**
   By embracing your true self, you align your thoughts, actions, and beliefs with your core values. This authenticity brings a sense of inner peace and contentment. No longer burdened by the need to conform, you can live a life true to yourself, free from the constant struggle of trying to be someone you're not. Embracing your true self allows you to let go of societal expectations and embrace your uniqueness with confidence.

2. **Increased Self-Awareness and Clarity:**
   Embracing your true self requires self-reflection and introspection. Through this process, you gain a deeper understanding of your passions, strengths, and weaknesses. Self-awareness allows you to make conscious choices aligned with your true desires, leading to a clearer sense of purpose and direction in life. You can set meaningful goals and make decisions that bring you closer to your authentic self.

3. **Increased Happiness and Life Satisfaction:**
   Living in alignment with your true self brings a profound sense of joy and fulfillment. When you pursue your passions and engage in activities that resonate with your authentic self, you experience a heightened sense of satisfaction. You find yourself engaged in pursuits that truly bring you happiness, rather than simply going through the motions of what society dictates. Embracing your true self allows you to live a life that is meaningful to you, fostering a lasting sense of contentment.

4. **Transformation:**
   Embracing your true self is a transformative journey of personal growth. By stepping into your authenticity, you continuously evolve and expand your horizons. Embracing your true self encourages you to challenge limiting beliefs and step outside of your comfort zone. As you embrace new experiences and embrace your true potential, you unlock untapped abilities and discover the depths of your resilience.

In conclusion, embracing your true self is not only a personal journey of self-discovery and acceptance, but it is also a revolutionary act of empowerment. It is a declaration that you refuse to be confined by societal norms and expectations. By embracing your true self, you tap into your authentic power, and you give yourself permission to shine brightly in the world. Remember, you are unique, with a combination of talents, perspectives, and passions that no one else possesses. When you embrace your true self, you unlock the potential to make a positive impact on the world around you. Your authenticity becomes a catalyst for change, as you inspire others to step into their own truth. Embracing your true self may not always be easy. It requires vulnerability, courage, and perseverance. There may be obstacles and moments of doubt along the way. But trust in your journey and have faith in your innate worthiness. You are deserving of love, happiness, and fulfillment, simply by being true to yourself. Embracing your true self is an ongoing process, a lifelong commitment to honouring who you are. It is about choosing authenticity over conformity, self-love over self-doubt, and courage over fear. So, step boldly into the world as your true self, and watch as the world opens its arms to embrace you in return.

II. Overcoming Self-Doubt and Fear of Judgment

Let's embark on a transformative journey, focusing on something that affects us all at some point in our lives: self-doubt and the fear of judgement. These formidable adversaries often hinder us from reaching our true potential, but fear not, for I am here to guide you toward reclaiming your confidence and embracing your inner strength. Together, we will explore practical strategies and empowering perspectives to overcome these obstacles. Remember, you are not alone in this battle, and with perseverance and self-belief, you can rise above your doubts and judgments. Self-doubt can creep into our minds, leaving us questioning our abilities, worth, and potential. It stems from various sources, such as past failures, external criticisms, or comparisons with others. To conquer self-doubt, we must first understand its origins and recognize that it is a common human experience. Acknowledge that everyone faces moments of uncertainty and that it doesn't define your capabilities or potential for growth.

You see, self-doubt is something that affects each and every one of us at some point in our lives. It's that nagging voice inside your head that questions your abilities, worth, and potential. But here's the thing: you are not alone in this experience. You're just like everyone else, face moments of uncertainty and questioning. It's a normal part of being human. So, let's take a moment to acknowledge that. By recognizing that self-doubt is a shared experience, you can begin to understand that it doesn't define who you are or what you're capable of achieving. Remember, you have unique qualities, talents, and perspectives that make you who you are. Your journey is different from anyone else's. By embracing this truth, you can start to let go of the comparisons and judgments that fuel self-doubt. Instead, focus on your strengths and the progress you've made. Celebrate the small victories along the way, for they are stepping stones to your growth.

It's important to understand that self-doubt often originates from past failures or external criticisms. But here's the secret: you have the power to shift your perspective. Rather than viewing mistakes as failures, consider them as opportunities for learning and growth. Allow yourself to make mistakes, because they are an integral part of your journey toward success. Lastly, remember that the judgments of others are often a reflection of their own insecurities and limited understanding. Surround yourself with supportive individuals who uplift and inspire you. Seek out people who genuinely believe in you and your potential. Their encouragement will help drown out the noise of doubt.

Now I'd like you to take a moment to understand that self-doubt is a normal part of life. But it doesn't have to define you. Embrace your uniqueness, celebrate your achievements, and surround yourself with positive influences. You are capable of so much more than you realize. Trust in yourself and your abilities, and watch as self-doubt gradually loses its grip on your life.

Self-compassion is another powerful tool in overcoming self-doubt. Treat yourself with kindness, understanding, and forgiveness. Instead of berating yourself for perceived shortcomings, practice self-care and self-acceptance. Celebrate your achievements, no matter how small, and remind yourself that you are deserving of love and respect. By nurturing self-compassion, you will build resilience and develop a stronger sense of self. At times, fear of judgement arises from the desire to conform to societal expectations or the need for external validation. However, the path to overcoming this fear lies in embracing your authenticity. Understand that you have unique qualities, talents, and perspectives that make you who you are. By embracing your true self and living in alignment with your values, you will attract genuine connections and build the self-assurance necessary to face any judgement that may come your way.

To conquer self-doubt and fear of judgement, it is crucial to shift your perspective. Instead of viewing mistakes as failures, see them as opportunities for growth and learning. Recognize that the judgments of others are often a reflection of their own insecurities and limited understanding. Surround yourself with supportive individuals who uplift and inspire you. Remember, you have the power to choose whose opinions truly matter in your life. Let's talk more about shifting perspectives, something that can truly empower you on your journey of overcoming self-doubt. You, my friend, have the incredible ability to change how you view yourself and the world around you. It's all about taking control of your thoughts and choosing to see things in a different light.

When it comes to self-doubt, it's easy to get caught up in negative thoughts and beliefs about yourself. But here's the thing: you have the power to challenge those beliefs and shift your perspective. Instead of seeing your mistakes as failures, you can view them as valuable lessons and opportunities for growth. Embrace a mindset of continuous improvement, knowing that each step forward, no matter how small, brings you closer to your goals.

Another important aspect of shifting perspectives is realizing that the judgments of others say more about them than they do about you. Often, people's opinions and criticisms are rooted in their own insecurities and limited understanding. So, rather than internalizing those judgments, remind yourself that you are the one who truly knows your worth and potential. Surround yourself with supportive and positive influences who believe in you and uplift your spirits. Remember, you have the power to choose whose opinions truly matter in your life. Focus on the people who genuinely support and inspire you, and let go of the weight of judgement from those who bring you down. By shifting your perspective and surrounding yourself with positive influences, you create a nurturing environment for self-belief and growth.

Embrace the power of shifting perspectives. Challenge negative beliefs, view mistakes as opportunities, and let go of the judgments that don't serve you. Trust in your own judgement and surround yourself with positivity. You are capable of incredible things, and by shifting your perspective, you'll unlock a world of possibilities and see yourself in a whole new light. What are those questions you often ask yourself in terms of seeking for opportunity that ad self-doubt? You always doubt your ability to become that person you've always wanted to become. Do you want to become an entrepreneur Or lawyer? What is that thing you want to become? Believe me, they're not far from you but you let self-doubt overshadow your dreams. Right, take a moment and write down those questions you always ask yourself whenever you want to do something great for yourself.

Certainly here are some questions you often ask yourself when faced with opportunity with will change your entire life:

1. What skills or strengths do I possess that are relevant to these opportunities?
2. I am not worthy of this position compared to others, I can't, I'm not capable. What if I get rejected?

How can I shift my focus to my own progress and growth?
3. What are my past accomplishments or successes that demonstrate my abilities?
4. What evidence do I have to prove that I'm qualified for this position?

Certainly! Here are the answers to the questions you always asked yourself:

1. I have strong problem-solving skills, excellent communication abilities, and a good work ethic. I also have knowledge and experience in this particular area, which makes me qualified to handle these opportunities.
2. Yes, I often compare myself to others and feel inadequate. To shift my focus, I will remind myself that everyone has their own journey and that I should focus on my own progress and growth. I will set realistic goals for myself and measure my success based on my own improvements.
3. I successfully completed a challenging project at work that received recognition from my colleagues and superiors. I have also received positive feedback from clients for my skills and expertise.
4. I have achieved several significant milestones and successes in the past. People have praised my abilities and talents, which indicates that I am capable of doing well.

After writing your self-doubt questions down with its answers, now go ahead and remind yourself that you're not a failure. Now, go forth with confidence and let your light shine brightly, inspiring others along the way. The journey may not always be easy, but remember that you are not alone. You have the power to overcome self-doubt and fear of judgement, and I am here cheering you on every step of the way. Now, let's dive into the exhilarating realm of taking action and stepping outside your comfort zone, because this is where true transformation happens, my friend. You, yes you, have the power to push past your limitations and discover the incredible growth that lies just beyond your comfort zone. Here's the thing: staying within the boundaries of what feels safe and familiar might seem comforting, but it also keeps you from reaching your full potential. Growth happens when you stretch yourself and venture into uncharted territory. So, I encourage you to take that first step, no matter how small, outside of what feels comfortable. You might be wondering, "Why should I do this?" Well, here's why: by taking action and stepping outside your comfort zone, you challenge your self-doubt and prove to yourself that you are capable of more than you thought. It's about expanding your horizons, acquiring new skills, and discovering strengths you didn't know you had. Start by setting achievable goals that push you just beyond your current limits. Maybe it's speaking up in a meeting or trying out a new hobby. As you achieve these smaller goals, you'll gain confidence and momentum to tackle bigger challenges. Remember, growth happens outside of your comfort zone. Embrace the discomfort as a sign that you're on the right path. It might feel scary at first, but trust me, the rewards are worth it. And don't worry about making mistakes along the way. They are simply stepping stones to success and valuable lessons that will propel you forward. Surround yourself with a supportive community that encourages and inspires you. Seek mentors or role models who have faced similar challenges and succeeded. Their guidance and encouragement will give you the strength to persevere and keep pushing beyond your comfort zone. I challenge you to take action today. Step outside your comfort zone and embark on the journey of self-discovery and growth. Start with small steps and gradually increase the level of difficulty. Each achievement, no matter how small, will reinforce your belief in yourself and silence the doubts that hold you back. Remember, you are capable of great things. Embrace the unknown, embrace the discomfort, and watch as your confidence soars and your potential expands. It's time to unlock the amazing possibilities that await you just outside your comfort zone.

In conclusion, you have embarked on a courageous journey of overcoming self-doubt and fear of judgement. Throughout this process, you have discovered that these adversaries do not define you or your potential. You have learned powerful strategies and perspectives to reclaim your confidence and embrace your inner strength. Remember that self-doubt is a natural part of the human experience, but it does not have to hold you back. Embrace your authenticity, shift your perspective, cultivate self-compassion, and take action. Surround yourself with a supportive community that uplifts and celebrates your growth. Believe in your abilities and trust that you have the strength to overcome any obstacle. As you continue on your path of self-discovery, know that you are worthy, resilient, and capable of achieving greatness. Embrace your uniqueness and celebrate your achievements, no matter how small. Surround yourself with positive influences that believe in your potential. Trust in yourself and your abilities, and watch as self-doubt gradually loses its grip on your life. Embrace the power of shifting perspectives and challenge negative beliefs. View mistakes as opportunities for growth and learning. Let go of judgments that don't serve you, and focus on the opinions of those who truly matter. Step outside your comfort zone, for it is where growth and transformation occur.

You are capable of extraordinary things. Embrace your inner strength, for it is the key to unlocking a world of limitless possibilities. Trust yourself, be kind to yourself, and keep moving forward with unwavering belief in your worth and potential.

III. Honouring Your Unique Path

A path that is intricately woven with your experiences, aspirations, and desires. It is a path that reflects your individuality, your dreams, and your purpose in life. Honouring your unique path means embracing all the facets that make you who you are, and cherishing the journey that unfolds before you. You are not meant to follow in someone else's footsteps. Your life is a canvas waiting to be painted with your own vibrant colours. The key to honouring your unique path lies in recognizing that you possess a special set of gifts, talents, and perspectives that no one else in this vast universe possesses. Embrace your strengths, your quirks, and your passions, for they are the very essence of what makes you unique. Celebrate the things that make your heart sing and your spirit soar. Whether it's your love for art, your knack for problem-solving, or your talent for connecting with others, these are the building blocks that shape your path. Remember, your path may not always be smooth. There will be obstacles, challenges, and moments of doubt along the way. But it is during these times that honouring your unique path becomes even more crucial. It is during these moments that you must tap into your inner strength, your resilience, and your unwavering belief in yourself. Comparing yourself to others is a tempting trap to fall into, but it only hinders your progress. Your journey is not a competition with anyone else's. It is a personal voyage of self-discovery and growth. Look within yourself and recognize the incredible potential that resides within. Embrace your own pace, for each step you take on your path is significant and worthy of celebration. Honouring your unique path also means listening to your intuition. Deep within you lies a guiding voice, a whisper of wisdom that knows what is best for you. Tune in to that voice, trust it, and let it lead you. Even when the world around you may seem chaotic or uncertain, your inner compass will guide you towards the right direction. Remember that your unique path is not set in stone. It is a living, breathing entity that evolves and transforms alongside you. Embrace change, for it is through change that you grow, learn, and discover new dimensions of yourself. Allow yourself the freedom to explore different avenues, to take detours, and to learn from every twist and turn. Lastly, honour your unique path by staying true to yourself. In a world that often tries to mould individuals into predefined boxes, dare to be authentically you. Embrace your quirks, your passions, and your dreams unapologetically. Your authenticity is a powerful force that will attract like-minded souls and open doors to opportunities you never thought possible. Honouring your unique path is a deeply personal and empowering journey. Here are some practical steps you can take to honour and embrace your individuality:

- **Celebrate milestones and achievements:** Take time to acknowledge and celebrate the milestones and achievements along your unique path. Recognize your progress, no matter how small, and reward yourself for the effort and dedication you've invested. Celebrating your accomplishments helps you stay motivated and reinforces the value of honouring your own journey.

- **Embrace uncertainty:** Recognize that life is filled with uncertainties and that your path may not always be clear. Embrace the unknown and trust that each step you take will lead you to where you need to be. Embracing uncertainty allows you to remain open to new opportunities and possibilities that may align with your unique path.

- **Let go of comparison:** Avoid comparing your journey to others. Each individual has their own unique path, and comparison can be a major hindrance to honouring your own. Focus on your progress, celebrate your accomplishments, and remember that your journey is incomparable and uniquely yours.

- **Embrace lifelong learning:** Cultivate a mindset of continuous learning and growth. Explore new interests, acquire new skills, and expand your knowledge. Engage in activities that stimulate your curiosity and broaden your perspectives. Lifelong learning enriches your unique path and opens doors to new opportunities.

- **Trust the timing of your life:** Trust that the timing of your unique path is perfect for you. Avoid comparing your journey to others or feeling pressured by societal timelines. Trust that you are exactly where you need to be in this moment, and that the unfolding of your path is happening in its own divine timing.

Honouring your unique path is a lifelong endeavour that requires self-awareness, self-compassion, and a willingness to embrace the unknown. By incorporating these practices into your life, you will continue to grow, evolve, and create a fulfilling and authentic journey that is uniquely yours. In conclusion, honouring your unique path is a deeply personal and transformative journey. It requires self-reflection, authenticity, self-compassion, and a willingness to embrace change and uncertainty. By embracing your true self, setting meaningful goals, trusting your intuition, and surrounding yourself with supportive individuals, you can navigate your path with confidence and purpose. Remember to celebrate your accomplishments, learn from challenges, and cultivate resilience along the way. Embrace the beauty of lifelong learning, and let go of comparison to others. Trust in the timing of your life, and have faith that every step you take is leading you towards a fulfilling and authentic existence. Your unique path is a testament to your individuality, strengths, and passions. It is a journey of self-discovery, growth, and self-expression. Embrace it wholeheartedly, for it is in honouring your unique path that you unlock your true potential and create a life that is aligned with your deepest desires and aspirations. So, I encourage you today to embark on this extraordinary journey with courage and an open heart. Trust in yourself, believe in the power of your unique path, and embrace the limitless possibilities that lie ahead. Your path is waiting for you to honour it, and as you do, you will discover a profound sense of purpose, fulfillment, and joy that only comes from living authentically as the remarkable individual you are.

CHAPTER FIVE

<u>Aligning Values and Actions</u>

"Success is not the key to happiness. Happiness is the key to success. If you love what you are doing, you will be successful." - Albert Schweitzer

Let's go into the fascinating issue of harmonising values and actions in this chapter. It's an essential aspect of personal growth and fulfillment that can transform your life.
Understanding how to bridge the gap between what you believe in and how you behave can empower you to live a more authentic and meaningful life. So, let's explore the significance of aligning your values with your actions and how you can make it happen.
First you start by defining your values, it's crucial to first understand what values are. Values are deeply held beliefs and principles that guide your thoughts, decisions, and actions. They reflect who you are and what you stand for, serving as a compass to navigate through life's challenges. Identifying your core values is the foundation for aligning them with your actions. Defining your values is like discovering the compass that guides your life's journey. It's about understanding what truly matters to you at the core. When we talk about values, we're referring to the principles and beliefs that shape your thoughts, decisions, and actions. Imagine yourself standing at a crossroad, unsure which path to take. Defining your values is like having a trustworthy map that helps you navigate through life's challenges and make choices that align with who you are. It's about discovering the fundamental aspects that give your life meaning and purpose. To define your values, it requires some introspection and self-reflection. You might ask yourself questions such as: What principles do I hold dear? What brings me the most joy and satisfaction in life? What beliefs do I hold that shape my worldview?
These inquiries encourage you to delve deeper into your inner self, exploring what truly resonates with you. Your values could revolve around honesty, compassion, integrity, creativity, freedom, justice, or any other principle that speaks to your heart. There are no right or wrong answers; it's about uncovering what feels genuine and authentic to you. Think of your values as the pillars upon which you build your life. They act as a compass, guiding your decisions and actions in both personal and professional domains. When you know your values, you gain clarity about what truly matters to you and what you want to prioritize in your life.
Once you identify your core values, they become your guiding light. They serve as a benchmark against which you can evaluate your actions and choices. When your actions align with your values, there is a sense of congruence and harmony within yourself. Defining your values is an ongoing process. As you grow and evolve, your values may also evolve with you. What was important to you in the past may not hold the same significance today. It's essential to periodically re-evaluate your values, ensuring that they still resonate with who you are becoming.

The misalignment dilemma is something many of us have experienced at some point in our lives. It's that feeling of discomfort or dissatisfaction when our actions don't align with our values. It's like having a nagging sense that something isn't quite right. Imagine this: You strongly believe in honesty and integrity, but you find yourself engaging in behaviors that compromise those values, perhaps bending the truth or acting in a way that goes against your principles. In such moments, you may experience a sense of inner conflict, a lack of fulfillment, and a feeling of being disconnected from your true self. The misalignment dilemma can arise due to various reasons. Sometimes, external pressures or societal expectations can influence our choices, causing us to deviate from our values. Other times, it might be our own fears, insecurities, or the desire to fit in that leads us astray. It's not always easy to swim against the current or go against what others expect of us. Living in this misalignment can be emotionally and mentally draining. It creates a sense of incongruence within ourselves. We may feel like we're wearing a mask, trying to please others or conform to societal norms, while deep down, we yearn for authenticity and integrity. Recognizing the misalignment dilemma is the first step towards growth and positive change. It requires honest introspection and reflection. Take the time to observe and question your actions in light of your values. Ask yourself: Are my behaviors in line with what I truly believe in? Am I compromising my values to meet external expectations or gain temporary benefits?

By acknowledging the misalignment, you open the door to self-awareness and the opportunity for transformation. It empowers you to make conscious choices that bring your actions into harmony with your values. It may involve making difficult decisions, setting boundaries, or finding ways to align your everyday behaviors with what you genuinely believe in. However, the rewards of aligning your values and actions are immense. When your actions align with your values, you experience a profound sense of authenticity, integrity, and fulfillment. You become more in tune with your true self, and you radiate a genuine aura that attracts like-minded individuals and opportunities into your life.

In the vibrant city of New York, there lived a determined and ambitious young man named Marcus Bennett. Growing up in a modest neighbourhood, Marcus dreamt of making a name for himself and leaving a lasting impact on the world. He was known among his friends as "Mr. Bigs" due to his big dreams and unwavering determination. From a young age, Marcus displayed remarkable leadership qualities. He was always the one organizing group activities, spearheading community projects, and encouraging his peers to reach for the stars. His infectious enthusiasm and charisma earned him respect and admiration.

As Marcus entered adulthood, his dreams grew even bigger. He had a burning desire to make a positive difference in the lives of others and contribute to society. He set out to establish his own nonprofit organization called "Mr. Bigs Foundation," dedicated to empowering underprivileged youth and providing them with opportunities for education and personal development. With relentless passion and hard work, Marcus built the foundation from the ground up. He collaborated with local schools, businesses, and volunteers to create mentorship programs, scholarships, and extracurricular activities that nurtured the talents and aspirations of young individuals who lacked resources. Under Marcus's guidance, the Mr. Bigs Foundation became a beacon of hope for countless young people. It offered them a support system, a platform to showcase their skills, and the tools to overcome obstacles. Marcus understood the importance of aligning his values with his actions, and he consistently led by example, inspiring both his team and the beneficiaries of the foundation. Over the years, the Mr. Bigs Foundation's impact grew exponentially. It expanded its reach beyond New York, reaching communities across the country. Marcus's dedication and unwavering belief in the potential of every young person touched the hearts of many, attracting support from influential individuals and organizations. As the years went by, Marcus never lost sight of his initial vision. He remained committed to ensuring that every child, regardless of their circumstances, had access to education, mentorship, and opportunities for personal growth. The Mr. Bigs Foundation became a lifeline for countless individuals who would have otherwise been left behind. Marcus, or "Mr. Bigs," as he was affectionately known, became an inspiration and role model for generations to come. His relentless pursuit of his dreams, coupled with his genuine desire to uplift others, left an indelible mark on the world. Through his actions, he proved that it is possible to align one's values with their actions and make a profound difference in the lives of others. And so, the story of Marcus Bennett, the young man who became "Mr. Bigs," stands as a testament to the power of unwavering determination, compassion, and the incredible impact one individual can have when they wholeheartedly pursue their dreams and align their values with their actions.

Now let's talk more about unveiling your values. Unveiling your values is like embarking on a journey of self-discovery, where you get to know yourself on a deeper level. It's about peeling back the layers and uncovering the core principles and beliefs that shape who you truly are. So, let's dive into the process of unveiling your values. Start by asking yourself thought-provoking questions. What principles do I hold dear? What qualities and virtues do I admire in others? What brings me the most joy and fulfillment in life? What deeply held beliefs shape my worldview? Allow yourself to explore these questions without judgement or expectation. As you delve into these inquiries, pay attention to your emotions and intuition. What values evoke a strong sense of alignment within you? Which ones resonate deeply and make you feel alive, inspired, and connected to your authentic self? Remember, there are no right or wrong answers. Your values are unique to you, reflecting your individuality and personal experiences. Imagine yourself opening a treasure chest filled with precious gems, each representing a value that resonates with your soul. Unveiling your values begins with introspection and reflection. Take some time to create a space for self-discovery, a moment to connect with your inner thoughts and emotions.

Sometimes, it can be helpful to reflect on significant moments in your life that have had a lasting impact. What values were present in those moments? What principles guided your actions and decisions during those times? These reflections can provide valuable insights into the values that are already woven into the fabric of your being. Another useful exercise is to envision your ideal life. What does a life lived in alignment with your values look like? How would you behave, make choices, and interact with others? This exercise helps you gain clarity on the values you aspire to embody and can serve as a guidepost in your journey.

It's important to note that unveiling your values is an ongoing process. As you grow and evolve, your values may also evolve with you. Therefore, it's crucial to periodically reassess and reevaluate your values, ensuring they still resonate with your current self.

Remember, unveiling your values is a personal exploration, and there's no rush or right answer. Embrace the journey of self-discovery and be patient with yourself along the way. Trust that the process will unfold organically, and as you unveil your values, you gain a deeper understanding of who you are and what truly matters to you.

Unveiling your values is an empowering endeavour. It provides you with a compass to navigate through life, making decisions and choices that are congruent with your authentic self. It enables you to live a life of purpose, meaning, and fulfillment, aligned with what truly matters to you at the core. So, take your time to unveil your values, and let them guide you on your path to self-discovery and a more authentic, purpose-driven life.

Bridging the gap between your values and actions is like building a sturdy bridge that connects who you are with how you live your life. It's the process of aligning your behaviors, choices, and decisions with the core principles and beliefs that you hold dear. So, let's explore how you can bridge the gap and create congruence between your values and actions. The first step in bridging the gap is to evaluate your current behaviors and choices. Take an honest look at how you are living your life. Ask yourself: Are my actions in line with my values? Do they reflect the principles and beliefs that I hold dear? This self-reflection is essential to identify areas where there might be discrepancies or misalignments. Once you've identified the areas where the gap exists, it's time to make adjustments. Remember, this process doesn't require you to completely overhaul your life overnight. Instead, focus on making small, consistent changes that align with your values. Rome wasn't built in a day, and similarly, bridging the gap takes time and effort.

Set clear goals that reflect your values. Break them down into actionable steps that you can take daily or weekly. For example, if one of your values is health, you might set a goal to exercise for 30 minutes each day or make healthier food choices. These small actions, when done consistently, accumulate over time and bridge the gap between your values and actions.

Developing new habits can also help bridge the gap. Habits are powerful because they automate our behaviors, making it easier to align our actions with our values. Choose habits that are in line with your values and make a commitment to practice them regularly. With dedication and persistence, these habits become ingrained, leading to a more congruent lifestyle.

In the process of bridging the gap, it's important to be mindful and aware of your actions. Cultivate a sense of self-observation and reflection. Regularly check in with yourself and ask: Am I acting in alignment with my values in this situation? This awareness helps you course-correct whenever you notice any deviations and reinforces the bridge you're building. Sometimes, bridging the gap may require making difficult choices. It might involve letting go of relationships, environments, or situations that contradict your values. It takes courage to make these choices, but remember that by staying true to your values, you create space for more fulfilling and authentic experiences to enter your life.

Surrounding yourself with supportive individuals who share your values can greatly assist in bridging the gap. Seek out communities, groups, or like-minded friends who can encourage and inspire you on your journey. Connecting with others who are also striving to align their values with their actions can provide a sense of accountability and support. Lastly, be patient and compassionate with yourself throughout the process. Bridging the gap is a continuous journey, and it's normal to encounter setbacks or moments when you might slip out of alignment. Embrace these experiences as opportunities for growth and learning, and use them to recalibrate and strengthen the bridge you're constructing. Bridging the gap between your values and actions is a transformative endeavour. It empowers you to live a more authentic, purpose-driven life, where your behaviors and choices are congruent with your core beliefs. By building this bridge, you create a solid foundation for personal growth, fulfillment, and a sense of wholeness. So, take the leap and begin bridging the gap between your values and actions. Embrace the process, make conscious choices, and celebrate each step forward. As you bridge the gap, you'll experience a greater sense of alignment, integrity, and joy in living a life that reflects who you truly are.

The ripple effect is a phenomenon that demonstrates the power of our actions and how they can create far-reaching impacts beyond ourselves. It's like dropping a pebble into a calm pond and watching as the ripples expand outward, touching everything in their path. When you align your values and actions, you become a living embodiment of what you believe in. Your words and behaviors are in harmony with your core principles, creating an authentic presence that inspires and influences those around you. People notice your integrity, your commitment to your values, and the congruence between what you say and what you do. Your actions have the power to inspire others to examine their own values and choices. When people witness the positive impact your values have on your life, they may be motivated to explore their own values and align their actions accordingly. This creates a ripple effect as others start to live more authentically and make choices that align with their core beliefs. Your relationships also benefit from the ripple effect of aligning values and actions. By living in congruence with your values, you foster deeper connections with others who share similar beliefs. Authenticity and integrity become the foundation of your interactions, leading to stronger and more meaningful relationships. As you stay true to your values, you attract like-minded individuals who appreciate and resonate with your authentic self.

Moreover, the ripple effect extends beyond your immediate circle. When you consistently align your values with your actions, your impact extends to the broader community. Your words, behaviors, and choices become catalysts for positive change, inspiring others to consider their own values and make conscious choices that benefit society as a whole. By living according to your values, you contribute to creating a more harmonious and compassionate society. You become a role model for others, showing them that it is possible to live in alignment with one's values and make a positive difference. Your actions ripple outwards, encouraging others to examine their own values, leading to a collective shift towards greater authenticity and social responsibility.

The ripple effect doesn't stop there. As more individuals embrace the power of aligning values and actions, the collective impact grows exponentially. A ripple started by one person can influence others, who, in turn, influence others, creating a ripple effect that spreads far and wide. Together, these ripples can create a tidal wave of positive change, shaping communities, institutions, and even the world at large. So, recognize the immense power of your actions and the ripple effect they can create. Embrace the opportunity to align your values with your actions, knowing that even the smallest choices can have profound impacts. Be the pebble that creates a ripple, inspiring others to live authentically, and contributing to a more compassionate and harmonious world. Remember, you have the power to make a difference. Your values and actions can create a ripple effect that surpasses boundaries and transforms lives. Embrace this power, live authentically, and let your positive actions send ripples of change throughout the world.

In conclusion, aligning values and actions is a transformative journey that empowers you to live a more authentic, purposeful, and fulfilling life. It involves bridging the gap between what you believe in and how you behave, creating a harmony between your core values and your everyday actions. By aligning your values and actions, you embark on a path of self-discovery, self-acceptance, and personal growth.

Throughout this process, remember that defining your values is the first step. Take the time to unveil and understand what truly matters to you at the core. Let your values serve as a compass, guiding your decisions, behaviors, and interactions with others. Embrace the ripple effect of aligning values and actions. Your authenticity and integrity inspire and influence those around you, creating a positive impact in your relationships, community, and beyond.

Your actions can be a catalyst for others to explore their own values and make positive changes in their lives.

Bridging the gap between your values and actions requires self-reflection, setting goals, developing new habits, and making conscious choices that align with your values. It may involve overcoming challenges and staying committed to living authentically, even in the face of external pressures or societal expectations.

Remember, this journey is ongoing. It requires patience, self-compassion, and a willingness to grow and evolve. Embrace the process, celebrate your progress, and be open to reevaluating your values as you continue to learn and change. By aligning your values and actions, you create a life that is congruent with your true self. You experience a deeper sense of fulfillment, purpose, and joy. You contribute to a more authentic and compassionate society, as your positive ripple effect extends far beyond what you can imagine. So, embrace the power within you to align your values and actions. Step into a life that reflects who you truly are and make a positive difference in the world. Live authentically, walk your talk, and let the journey of aligning values and actions be your guide to a truly meaningful and extraordinary life.

I. Discovering Your Core Values

You are a unique individual with a rich tapestry of experiences, beliefs, and aspirations that shape who you are. At the very core of your being lies a set of values that define your character, guide your decisions, and provide a compass for living a fulfilling life. In this exploration of self-discovery, we will delve into the four processes of uncovering your core values and understand their profound impact on shaping the authentic you.

1. Reflect on Your Life Journey:

Reflecting on your life journey is like taking a step back and examining the significant moments and experiences that have shaped who you are today. It's a chance to dive into the chapters of your life, recalling the highs, lows, and everything in between.
Take a moment to reflect on your life journey, recalling significant events, relationships, and moments that have left a lasting impact on you. Consider the times when you felt most alive, fulfilled, and aligned with your true self. What values were present during those moments? These instances serve as clues, hinting at the values that resonate deeply with your being. Imagine closing your eyes and allowing your mind to wander through the timeline of your life. Think about the people you've met, the places you've been, and the adventures you've embarked upon. Remember the milestones, both big and small, that have left a lasting impact on you. These could be moments of triumph, moments of deep connection, or even moments of struggle and growth. As you reflect on your life journey, pay attention to the emotions and feelings that arise within you. What were the instances that made you feel alive, fulfilled, and aligned with your true self? Perhaps it was a time when you achieved a personal goal, overcame a challenge, or experienced a profound connection with someone. These moments hold valuable clues about the values that are at the core of your being. You may also want to ponder the lessons you've learned along the way. What insights have you gained from your experiences? Have there been any recurring themes or patterns that have shaped your perspective? By examining these lessons, you can start to uncover the principles and beliefs that have guided your journey. Reflecting on your life journey is an opportunity to gain a deeper understanding of who you are and what matters most to you. It allows you to connect the dots between your past experiences and your present self. So take a moment to delve into the memories, emotions, and lessons that have shaped you, for it is within these reflections that you will discover the treasures of your core values.

2. Identify Your Beliefs and Convictions:

Identifying your beliefs and convictions is like peering into the core of your being, uncovering the principles and ideals that you hold dear. These are the guiding lights that shape your thoughts, actions, and decisions.
Your beliefs and convictions form an integral part of your core values. Pay attention to the principles you hold dear and the ideals you strive to uphold. Think about what you stand for and the causes you are passionate about. Are you driven by justice, compassion, creativity, or integrity? By examining your convictions, you can begin to unveil the values that underpin your actions and choices. Think about the principles and values that you deeply believe in. Consider the causes, ideas, or philosophies that resonate with you on a profound level. It

could be a belief in justice, equality, honesty, compassion, or any other value that holds personal significance to you.

Take a moment to reflect on the convictions that have shaped your worldview. What do you stand for? What are the non-negotiables in your life? These beliefs are like anchors, grounding you in your truth and influencing the choices you make. Consider the moments in your life when you felt compelled to take a stand, when you passionately defended a cause or spoke up for what you believed was right. These instances offer valuable insights into the values that underpin your actions and decisions.

Your beliefs and convictions are unique to you, forged through your experiences, upbringing, and personal reflections. They reflect the essence of who you are and what you hold as important. By identifying and understanding your beliefs and convictions, you gain clarity on what matters most to you and can live in alignment with your authentic self.

It is important to remember that beliefs and convictions are not fixed and unchanging. They can evolve and grow as you gain new insights and experiences. So, be open to questioning and examining your beliefs from time to time. This process of self-reflection allows you to refine and strengthen your convictions, ensuring that they remain true to your evolving self. Identifying your beliefs and convictions is an empowering journey of self-discovery. It requires introspection, introspection, and a willingness to explore the depths of your values. By recognizing and honouring your beliefs, you lay the foundation for living a life that aligns with your deepest convictions, leading to a sense of fulfillment, purpose, and authenticity.

3. Observe Your Reactions and Emotional Responses:

Observing your reactions and emotional responses is like becoming an attentive observer of your own inner world. It involves paying close attention to how you feel and react in different situations, as these emotional cues can provide valuable insights into your core values. Emotions are powerful indicators of what truly matters to you. Notice the situations or experiences that evoke strong emotional responses within you. Do you feel outrage when witnessing injustice? Do acts of kindness make your heart swell with joy? Emotional reactions can offer valuable insights into the values that are at the core of your being. Pay close attention to these cues as they guide you towards understanding yourself better.

Picture yourself as a curious explorer, taking note of the emotions that arise within you throughout the day. Notice the moments when you feel a surge of joy, excitement, or passion. These emotions often signal that you are in alignment with something that deeply resonates with you.

Similarly, be aware of the instances when you experience discomfort, frustration, or anger. These emotional responses can indicate a clash between your values and the circumstances or actions around you. They serve as reminders that something important to you is being challenged or compromised.

Ask yourself: What values might be connected to these emotional reactions? For example, if witnessing an act of injustice sparks a deep sense of outrage within you, it could indicate that fairness and equality are core values you hold dear. If acts of kindness warm your heart and fill you with joy, it may reflect the value of compassion and empathy in your life.

By observing your emotional responses, you can uncover the values that are at the heart of who you are. Your emotions serve as messengers, signaling what matters to you on a deep, subconscious level. They provide valuable clues about the values you hold and can guide you in making choices that align with your authentic self.

Remember, emotions are not meant to be judged as good or bad. Instead, they are signals that provide you with valuable information about your values and the impact of your experiences. Embracing and understanding your emotional responses allows you to navigate life with greater self-awareness and make decisions that honour your truest self. Observe how they ebb and flow, and reflect on the values they may be connected to. Embrace your emotions as a powerful compass, guiding you towards a life that is in harmony with your core values and ultimately leading to a greater sense of fulfillment and authenticity.

4. Prioritize What Matters Most to You:

Prioritizing what matters most to you is like shining a spotlight on the aspects of your life that hold the deepest significance. It involves consciously identifying and giving importance to the values, relationships, goals, and experiences that truly resonate with your heart and soul. When you think about what truly matters in your life, what comes to mind? Consider the aspects that hold the most significance for you personally, be it relationships, personal growth, adventure, or making a difference in the world. Imagine if you had to choose only a few values to live by. Which ones would you prioritize above all else? Identifying your top values helps you align your actions and decisions with what you hold most. Imagine sitting down with a pen and paper, ready to create a personalized roadmap for your life. Start by reflecting on what brings you the greatest joy, fulfillment, and a sense of purpose. What activities or endeavours make you feel alive and engaged? Is it nurturing your relationships, pursuing a creative passion, making a positive impact on others, or dedicating time to self-care?
Consider the people and relationships that hold a special place in your heart. Who are the individuals that bring out the best in you? Whose presence uplifts and inspires you? Take a moment to think about how you can nurture and prioritize these connections, as they contribute to your overall well-being and happiness.
Additionally, ponder the goals and aspirations that you long to achieve. What dreams do you hold close to your heart? Whether they are related to career, personal growth, health, or contribution to society, these goals are the markers that shape the path you wish to traverse. Now, imagine you are faced with the challenge of choosing only a few values or aspects to focus on. Which ones would you prioritize above all else? These are the pillars that define your essence and serve as guiding principles in decision-making. They act as a filter through which you can evaluate opportunities, activities, and commitments. By consciously prioritizing what matters most to you, you create a sense of alignment and harmony in your life. You ensure that your time, energy, and resources are directed towards the things that truly resonate with your core values and bring you a deep sense of fulfillment.
Keep in mind that priorities may evolve over time as you grow, learn, and experience new chapters of life. Stay open to reassessing and realigning your priorities periodically, allowing yourself the freedom to adapt as you evolve.
In conclusion, discovering your core values is an introspective and transformative process that empowers you to live a life true to yourself. It is a journey of self-discovery that requires reflection, observation, and alignment with what truly matters to you. By identifying your core values, you gain a profound understanding of your authentic self, allowing you to make conscious choices that align with your deepest convictions and beliefs. Embracing your core values serves as a compass, guiding you through life's challenges and opportunities. When you prioritize what truly matters to you, you create a sense of purpose and meaning in

everything you do. Your core values become the foundation upon which you build your relationships, pursue your goals, and make decisions that align with your innermost desires. Moreover, discovering your core values is not a one-time process but a lifelong journey. As you grow, evolve, and experience new aspects of life, your values may shift and transform. Embrace this growth and allow yourself the freedom to reevaluate and realign your values accordingly. By remaining open to change, you ensure that your values continue to resonate with the person you are becoming. Remember, your core values are unique to you. They reflect your individuality, beliefs, and passions. Embrace them wholeheartedly, for they are the essence of you. Let them guide you towards a life that is fulfilling, authentic, and in harmony with your true self. Discovering your core values is a powerful step towards living a life that resonates with your true essence. Embrace the journey, embrace yourself, and let your core values be the guiding light that illuminates your path towards a meaningful and purposeful existence.

II. <u>Living in Alignment with Your Values</u>

At the heart of this journey lies the quest to live in alignment with your values, an endeavour that will empower you to embrace authenticity and lead a purposeful life. In this exploration, we will delve into the significance of understanding your values, identifying ways to align them with your actions, and the transformative impact this will have on your overall well-being.

Aligning Your Values with Your Actions.
Understanding your values is a powerful first step, but true transformation comes when you bridge the gap between knowing and doing. You must align your actions with your values, ensuring that the decisions you make in your daily life reflect what you hold dear. This alignment begins by recognizing that every choice you make, whether big or small, has an impact on your well-being and the lives of those around you. For instance, if you prioritize health and well-being, make a conscious effort to engage in regular exercise and nourish your body with wholesome foods. If you value honesty, be truthful with yourself and others, even when it's challenging. By actively living in alignment with your values, you'll experience a profound sense of congruence, purpose, and inner peace.

You know, aligning your values with your actions is all about living in harmony with your true self. It's about making sure that what you believe in your heart is reflected in the way you live your life. When your actions are in line with your values, you experience a sense of congruence and authenticity that brings a deep sense of fulfillment. Imagine this: You have certain beliefs and principles that guide your decisions, the way you treat others, and the goals you pursue. Let's say one of your core values is honesty. You genuinely believe in being truthful, both to yourself and to others. Now, if you align your actions with this value, it means you're being honest in all your interactions, even when it's challenging. You're not just saying you value honesty; you're actively living it.

It's like having a compass that always points you in the right direction. Whenever you face a choice or a decision, you can ask yourself, "Does this align with my values?" If the answer is yes, you'll feel confident and at peace with your choice. If the answer is no, it might be time to reassess and find a path that aligns better with what you hold dear. Sometimes, aligning your values with your actions can require courage. You might face situations where staying true to your beliefs means going against the crowd or standing up for what you believe in. It's not always easy, but the rewards are worth it. When you act in alignment with your values, you build a strong sense of self and self-respect, which, in turn, enhances your relationships and your overall well-being.

Another way to look at it is by thinking about your actions as a reflection of who you are on the inside. You don't just talk the talk; you walk the walk. For example, if you value kindness, you actively look for ways to be kind to others in your daily life. It could be a simple gesture, like holding the door for someone or offering a helping hand when needed.

Remember, living in alignment with your values is a journey. It's not about being perfect all the time. It's about being aware of your values, making an effort to live by them, and being compassionate with yourself when you stumble. Nobody's perfect, and that's okay. What matters is that you're committed to growing, learning, and becoming the best version of yourself.

By aligning your values with your actions, you create a life that feels authentic, purposeful, and fulfilling. You'll find a deeper sense of contentment and joy because you're living in harmony with your true self. So, take some time to reflect on what truly matters to you, identify your core values, and start making choices that align with them. Your journey towards living authentically and in line with your values begins with small steps, and each step brings you closer to a life of meaning and significance. Embrace this beautiful journey, and let your values guide you towards a life well-lived.

Resisting External Influences.

Resisting external influences is all about staying true to yourself and not letting outside pressures or expectations dictate your choices and actions. It's about maintaining your authenticity and individuality, even when the world around you tries to pull you in different directions. Picture this: You have your own set of values, beliefs, and dreams that make you who you are. They're like a compass that guides you on your journey through life. But sometimes, external influences, like societal norms, peer pressure, or the media, can attempt to sway you from your true path.

As you endeavour to live in alignment with your values, you will encounter external influences that might challenge your resolve. Society, media, and peer pressure may attempt to steer you away from your true self and towards conformity. Remember, staying true to your values is about honouring yourself and your individuality, rather than succumbing to external expectations. Maintaining alignment requires courage and resilience, but it is the path to cultivating a life that reflects your innermost desires. Surround yourself with supportive individuals who respect and appreciate your authenticity, empowering you to remain steadfast on your journey.

Resisting external influences means having the strength and courage to stand firm in your convictions, even when it's not the popular choice or when others might not understand. For example, let's say you have a passion for art, but your family and friends pressure you to pursue a more "stable" career. Resisting external influences means staying true to your love for art and finding a way to integrate it into your life, despite the pressure to conform. It's essential to remember that your journey is unique, and what works for others may not necessarily work for you. By resisting external influences, you give yourself the freedom to explore your own path and follow your heart's desires. It's about trusting your instincts and having confidence in your decisions.

Now, that's not to say that you should close yourself off to advice or new perspectives. Being open to learning and growth is vital, but the key is to filter external input through the lens of your values and what aligns with your authentic self.

Resisting external influences can be challenging at times, especially when it feels like the world is pushing you in a different direction. But remember, you have the power to choose what you allow to influence you and what you don't. Surrounding yourself with supportive and understanding people who respect your choices can also make a significant difference. Living in alignment with your values and resisting external influences go hand in hand. When you stay true to your core beliefs, it becomes easier to resist pressures that don't align with who you are. It empowers you to make choices that are genuine and fulfilling, leading to a more authentic and purpose-driven life.

Embracing Change and Growth.

Embracing change and growth is a fundamental aspect of personal development and a journey of continuous self-improvement. It's about welcoming the opportunities that come with change, and seeing it as a chance to evolve, learn, and seeing it as a chance to evolve, learn, and become a better version of yourself.

 Let's talk more about this exciting concept! Embracing change means being open to new experiences and perspectives. Life is full of twists and turns, and change is inevitable. Sometimes it might feel uncomfortable or even scary, but it's in those moments of change that we have the most potential for growth.

Think about it like this: Just as a caterpillar transforms into a beautiful butterfly, change gives you the chance to shed old habits, beliefs, and limitations, and emerge as a stronger, wiser, and more resilient individual.

When you embrace change, you let go of the fear of the unknown and step into the realm of possibilities. Instead of resisting change and holding onto the familiar, you welcome it with an open heart, ready to embrace the growth and opportunities it brings.

Now, growth goes hand in hand with change. It's about constantly seeking ways to improve yourself and expand your horizons. Growth isn't limited to a particular phase of life; it's a lifelong journey that enriches every aspect of who you are.

Embracing change and growth means having a growth mindset - seeing challenges as opportunities for learning and improvement rather than setbacks. It's about approaching life with curiosity, courage, and a willingness to step outside your comfort zone.

It's essential to be kind to yourself during this process. Embracing change and growth doesn't mean you have to have it all figured out from the start. It's okay to take one step at a time, to stumble, and to learn from your experiences. Every step forward, no matter how small, is progress towards a more fulfilling and meaningful life.

By embracing change and growth, you become adaptable and resilient, better equipped to navigate life's challenges with grace and determination. You realize that you have the power to shape your destiny, and that every day is an opportunity to grow, learn, and become a better version of yourself.

As you continue on your path of living in alignment with your values, you will experience growth and change. Embrace these moments wholeheartedly, for they signify your evolution into a more authentic version of yourself. You might find that some of your values evolve over time, and that is perfectly normal.

Stay open to reassessing and refining your values as you gain new perspectives and life experiences. Growth is an ongoing process, and it is through this evolution that you will unlock the full potential of living in harmony with your true self. So, embrace change as a catalyst for growth, and welcome the unknown with excitement. Trust in your ability to adapt and thrive, and believe in your capacity to handle whatever life throws your way. Embrace the journey of change and growth with an open heart, and you'll discover a world of possibilities and endless potential for personal transformation. Remember, you are capable of evolving and becoming the best version of yourself, and each step you take on this journey is a testament to your courage and determination.

Navigating Challenges and Finding Fulfillment.
Navigating challenges and finding fulfillment is an integral part of life's journey, and it's a journey we all go through together. It's about embracing the ups and downs, and learning to navigate through the obstacles that come your way while still finding joy and purpose in your experiences.

Let's dive into this topic together! Life is a series of challenges and opportunities, and it's how we handle these challenges that shapes our sense of fulfillment. When faced with difficulties, it's normal to feel overwhelmed or unsure, but remember that you have the strength and resilience to overcome them.

These challenges may be personal, professional, or even related to relationships. But every challenge presents a chance to grow, learn, and become a stronger individual. Navigating challenges means embracing a positive mindset. Instead of viewing obstacles as roadblocks, try seeing them as stepping stones toward growth. Challenges are opportunities for self-discovery and self-improvement. They teach you valuable life lessons and build your character.

Now, let's talk about fulfillment. Fulfillment comes from living a life that aligns with your values and passions. It's about finding meaning and purpose in your everyday experiences, no matter how big or small. Fulfillment isn't something that can be bought or achieved by reaching a particular goal; it's a state of being that comes from within.

Finding fulfillment means recognizing and appreciating the blessings and joys in your life, even amidst challenges. It's about being grateful for the journey and finding contentment in the present moment. When you align your actions with your values, you create a life that feels authentic and purposeful, and that's where true fulfillment lies.

When navigating challenges, it's essential to be kind to yourself. It's okay to have setbacks or moments of doubt - we all experience them. But remember that each challenge you overcome brings you closer to a sense of achievement and fulfillment.

Let's say you're facing a tough decision or a setback in your career. Navigating this challenge means taking a step back, reassessing your goals and values, and finding a way to move forward that aligns with who you are. It might involve seeking support from loved ones, mentors, or seeking professional guidance.

By approaching challenges with a growth mindset and a willingness to learn, you'll develop the resilience needed to navigate through them successfully. As you overcome challenges, you'll gain a deeper understanding of yourself and your capabilities, building your confidence in the process.

Remember, finding fulfillment isn't about avoiding challenges; it's about embracing them and using them as stepping stones towards a more purposeful and meaningful life. Each challenge you navigate brings you closer to a life that reflects your true self and brings you joy and contentment.

Living in alignment with your values does not shield you from life's challenges, but it equips you with a resilient mindset to face them. You will encounter obstacles that may test your commitment, but your strong sense of purpose will guide you through difficult times.

As you persist on this transformative journey, you will find that fulfillment is not a fleeting emotion but a sustained state of being. A life lived in alignment with your values enables you to experience genuine joy, contentment, and a profound sense of purpose that goes beyond fleeting moments of happiness.

Cultivating a Fulfilling Career.
Cultivating a fulfilling career is about finding a sense of purpose and satisfaction in your work, something that brings you joy and allows you to utilize your unique strengths and talents. It's a journey of self-discovery and growth, where your career becomes more than just a job—it becomes an extension of who you are and what you believe in. Imagine waking up every day, excited and eager to go to work because you genuinely love what you do. Cultivating a fulfilling career means finding a job or profession that aligns with your passions and values, and that brings a sense of fulfillment and contentment.

You might wonder, "How do I find a fulfilling career?" Well, it begins with self-reflection. Take some time to explore what truly makes you happy and what sparks your curiosity. What are your strengths, skills, and interests? Reflect on the activities that bring you joy and the tasks that energize you.

Once you have a better understanding of your passions and strengths, think about how you can align them with your career choices. Maybe you have a talent for writing and a deep love for environmental issues; perhaps a career in environmental journalism or sustainable marketing could be a perfect fit.

It's important to remember that a fulfilling career isn't always about landing the dream job from the start. It's a journey of growth and exploration, and sometimes it takes time to find the right path. Be open to trying new things and exploring different opportunities. Each experience is a chance to learn and grow, bringing you closer to a fulfilling career.

In your quest for a fulfilling career, seek out mentors and professionals in fields that interest you. Network, attend workshops, and gain insights from those who have already found success in areas you're passionate about. Their guidance can provide valuable advice and perspective on your career journey.

Furthermore, never underestimate the power of perseverance and dedication. Pursuing a fulfilling career may come with challenges and setbacks, but remember that each hurdle is an opportunity to learn and refine your path. Stay committed to your values and passions, and trust that your dedication will lead you to the right opportunities.

Cultivating a fulfilling career also means continuously investing in your growth and development. Stay curious, seek out learning opportunities, and embrace change. The job market and industries evolve, and staying adaptable ensures that you remain relevant and fulfilled throughout your career.

Lastly, remember that a fulfilling career isn't just about personal success—it's also about making a positive impact on others and the world around you. Consider how your unique skills and passions can contribute to solving real-world problems or making a difference in your community. In the end, a fulfilling career is the result of aligning your passions, values, and strengths with meaningful work. When you find that sweet spot where your career feels like a natural extension of who you are, you'll experience a profound sense of purpose and satisfaction. So, be true to yourself, stay open to new opportunities, and trust that with dedication and self-awareness, you can cultivate a fulfilling career that brings you joy, meaning, and a sense of accomplishment.

Transcending Materialism.

Transcending materialism is about moving beyond a sole focus on material possessions and recognizing that true happiness and fulfillment come from experiences, connections, and inner contentment. It's a shift in perspective that values the intangible aspects of life—such as love, growth, and personal well-being—over the pursuit of material wealth and possessions. Transcending materialism means recognizing that possessions alone do not define us, and there is so much more to life than what we own.

In our consumer-driven society, it's easy to get caught up in the allure of material possessions. We may believe that buying the latest gadgets, designer clothes, or expensive cars will bring us happiness and fulfillment. However, these external markers of success can only provide temporary satisfaction.

Transcending materialism is about finding contentment within ourselves, regardless of our possessions or external circumstances. It's recognizing that true happiness comes from within, from cultivating meaningful relationships, and from living in alignment with our values and passions. By focusing on experiences and connections, rather than possessions, we open ourselves up to a world of possibilities and a deeper sense of fulfillment. Think about the joy of spending quality time with loved ones, the satisfaction of accomplishing personal goals, or the wonder of exploring new places and cultures. These are the experiences that create lasting memories and enrich our lives.

It's not to say that material possessions are inherently bad, but rather that they should not be the sole source of our happiness or self-worth. Possessions can be enjoyed in moderation, but when we attach our sense of identity and happiness to what we own, we limit our potential for growth and genuine contentment.

Transcending materialism also involves letting go of the constant pursuit of more and embracing a simpler, more intentional lifestyle. It means being mindful of our consumption and focusing on what truly brings value to our lives.

To start transcending materialism, practice gratitude for what you already have and focus on the intangible aspects of life that truly matter. Cultivate meaningful relationships with others, engage in activities that bring you joy and fulfillment, and spend time on personal growth and self-discovery.

Consider the impact of your actions on the environment and society, and strive to make choices that align with your values and have a positive impact on the world around you. By focusing on what truly matters, you'll find that your life becomes more purposeful and satisfying. Remember, transcending materialism is a journey, and it's okay to take small steps towards change. Embrace the freedom that comes from shifting your perspective and find contentment in the richness of life beyond material possessions. By focusing on experiences, connections, and personal growth, you'll discover a deeper sense of fulfillment and joy that transcends the fleeting allure of materialism.

Finding Meaning and Purpose.

Finding meaning and purpose is about discovering the deeper significance and direction in your life. It's the quest to understand why you're here, what brings fulfillment to your existence, and how you can make a positive impact on the world around you. Finding meaning and purpose is a deeply personal and introspective journey that can lead to a more fulfilling and enriched life.

Finally, let's explore this journey together! Imagine waking up each day with a sense of direction and clarity, knowing that your actions are guided by a greater purpose. Finding meaning and purpose is like uncovering the hidden treasure within yourself—a treasure that gives your life profound significance and joy.

To begin this journey, take some time for self-reflection. Ask yourself what truly matters to you, what brings you joy and fulfillment, and what ignites a sense of passion within you. Reflect on your core values and beliefs, as they often hold valuable clues to your purpose. Sometimes, finding meaning and purpose involves exploring different experiences and opportunities. Be open to trying new things, stepping out of your comfort zone, and learning from each experience. Some people find their purpose through their careers, while others discover it through hobbies, volunteering, or relationships.

Consider what makes you feel alive, what makes time seem to fly, and what activities bring you a sense of flow—where you're fully immersed and deeply engaged in the present moment. These are often signs that you're aligning with your purpose. Finding meaning and purpose can also be connected to making a positive impact on others and the world. Think about the ways you can contribute to something bigger than yourself, whether it's through acts of kindness, advocacy for a cause, or supporting your community.

It's essential to understand that finding meaning and purpose is not a one-time event but an ongoing journey. As you grow and evolve, your sense of purpose may shift and expand. Embrace change, and be gentle with yourself if you don't have all the answers right away. Trust that the journey itself is a valuable part of the process.

Once you start uncovering your purpose, consider how you can integrate it into various aspects of your life. Infuse your daily actions, relationships, and decisions with meaning and intention. Living in alignment with your purpose brings a sense of fulfillment and coherence to your life. Remember that your purpose doesn't have to be grand or world-changing. It can be as simple as being a source of support and love for your family or dedicating yourself to a cause that's close to your heart. Ultimately, finding meaning and purpose is about connecting with your authentic self, understanding your values and passions, and embracing the journey of self-discovery. It's about living a life that reflects your true essence and making a positive impact on the world in your unique way. So, be patient and open-minded, and trust that the journey of finding meaning and purpose will lead you to a more meaningful and fulfilling life.

In conclusion, living in alignment with your values is not a destination but an ongoing journey of self-discovery, growth, and contribution to the world. It is a path that empowers you to embrace your authentic self, cultivate meaningful relationships, and make a positive impact on your surroundings. By understanding your core values, you gain a profound insight into what drives you, what brings you joy, and what truly matters in your life. As you embark on this transformative journey, remember that it is okay to take one step at a time. Living in alignment with your values is not about perfection or adhering to an external standard; it is about being true to yourself and honouring the unique person you are. Embrace the growth mindset, and view challenges as opportunities for learning and improvement. Living in alignment with your values requires courage, as it might mean making difficult choices or stepping away from societal norms. However, the rewards are immeasurable: a life filled with purpose, authenticity, and inner peace. Your commitment to authenticity will inspire others to do the same, fostering a ripple effect of positive change in the world. Through the integration of your values into your daily life, you create a harmonious union between your inner beliefs and your external actions. This integration brings forth a sense of congruence that permeates all aspects of your existence, leading to greater emotional well-being, enhanced resilience, and the ability to embrace life's challenges with grace.

As you navigate this journey, remember to be compassionate with yourself. Embrace your imperfections and celebrate your unique qualities. Each step taken in alignment with your values strengthens your connection with your true self and brings you closer to a life of genuine fulfillment and contentment. In this quest for authenticity, you leave behind a powerful legacy for those who come after you. By living in alignment with your values, you contribute to a world where empathy, compassion, and purpose-driven actions become the norm, inspiring future generations to build upon the foundation you have laid. So, embark on this extraordinary journey with confidence and curiosity. Embrace the power of your values to shape your life, and let them be your guiding light in times of doubt or uncertainty. Allow your authentic self to shine, for it is through this luminous authenticity that you create a life that not only reflects who you are but also positively impacts the world around you. Remember, you are the author of your story, and living in alignment with your values is the key to unlocking your full potential, igniting your passions, and leaving a lasting mark on the canvas of life. Embrace the beauty of authenticity, and savour each moment as you weave together a tapestry of purpose, connection, and fulfillment. The journey is yours, and the possibilities are boundless. So, step forward with courage, and may living in alignment with your values illuminate the path to a life of meaning and significance.

III. Creating Meaningful Goals and Intentions

Setting goals is an essential aspect of personal and professional growth, allowing you to direct your actions toward desired outcomes. When you embark on this process, you embark on a path of self-discovery and self-empowerment. In this exploration, you'll learn how to set clear and achievable objectives, align them with your values and passions, and stay motivated throughout the journey. Let's delve into the process of crafting meaningful goals and intentions tailored to your unique aspirations and intentions tailored to your unique aspirations and ambitions. To create meaningful goals, you must begin with introspection and self-awareness. Ask yourself, "What excites and motivates me?" Explore your interests, hobbies, and activities that bring you joy and fulfillment. Reflect on moments when you felt most alive and engaged. These passions will be the foundation for your goals and intentions. As you delve into your passions, consider your values and beliefs. What do you care deeply about? What principles guide your life decisions? Aligning your goals with your core values will provide a strong sense of purpose and ensure that your intentions are authentic to you. Once you've identified your passions and values, it's time to convert them into tangible goals. Make your goals specific and measurable, avoiding vague statements. Instead of saying, "I want to be successful," define what success means to you and set quantifiable benchmarks to track your progress.

For example, if you aspire to start your own business, a specific and measurable goal could be, "By the end of the year, I will launch my online store and have 500 customers." By setting clear objectives, you create a roadmap that helps you stay focused and committed to your aspirations. Achieving meaningful goals can be overwhelming, especially if they are ambitious. To prevent feeling discouraged, break each goal into smaller, manageable steps. This approach enables you to celebrate incremental achievements, keeping you motivated along the way. Let's take the previous example of starting a business. The smaller steps could include market research, creating a business plan, setting up a website, and developing a marketing strategy. Tackling these steps one by one will lead you closer to your ultimate goal. Accountability is crucial in pursuing your goals. Share your aspirations with friends, family, or a mentor who can provide support and encouragement. Regularly update them on your progress and discuss any challenges you encounter.

Throughout your journey, remember to celebrate every milestone, no matter how small. Acknowledge your efforts and accomplishments, as this positive reinforcement enhances your motivation and resilience.

Additionally, be kind to yourself when facing setbacks or moments of self-doubt. Practicing self-compassion ensures you treat yourself with the same kindness and understanding you would offer to a friend. It's normal to encounter challenges, and your ability to bounce back is a testament to your strength.

Creating meaningful goals and intentions is a transformative process that enables you to shape your future in alignment with your passions, values, and ambitions. By following these steps, you empower yourself to take charge of your life and embrace the journey of growth and self-discovery. Remember that setting goals is not just about reaching the destination but also relishing the process of growth and transformation along the way. Embrace the power of intentional goal-setting, and you'll find yourself living a more purposeful and fulfilling life.

Stay accountable, lean on your support system, and embrace the power of flexibility as you navigate the twists and turns of your journey. Celebrate your achievements, no matter how big or small, and practice self-compassion during moments of challenge. By dedicating yourself to this intentional process, you cultivate a life that resonates with authenticity and fulfillment. Remember, it is the pursuit of your aspirations that will mould your character and transform your existence. So, embark on this empowering journey with enthusiasm and determination, for the fulfillment of meaningful goals lies within your grasp. With each step you take, you shape a future that reflects the essence of who you truly are.

The path may not always be straightforward, but with your passions as a guiding compass and your intentions as a driving force, you are capable of achieving greatness beyond your wildest imagination.

Now, armed with the knowledge and inspiration gained from this exploration, go forth and craft your own meaningful goals and intentions. Your future is in your hands, and the possibilities are limitless.

CHAPTER SIX

Connecting with Others and Contributing to the World

"Your positive action combined with positive thinking results in success." - Shiv Khera

In this ever-changing world, one of the most significant aspects of life is the profound connection you share with others. From family and friends to acquaintances and strangers, the bonds you form shape your experiences, influence your perspectives, and enable you to contribute meaningfully to the world around you. Embracing this interconnectedness and recognizing the impact you can have on others can lead you to a fulfilling and purposeful life. Today, I want to take you on a journey through my personal experiences, illustrating how connecting with others and contributing to the world can enrich your existence and the lives of those you touch.

Certainly! You may be wondering how I got through this ever-changing world's obstacles and setbacks, but I'd like you to take 5 minutes to ask yourself these self-reflective questions to help you examine how you might better connect with others and contribute to the world. Now after questioning yourself, brainstorming your thoughts and reflecting on the person you'd always wanted to become, get a booklet and write all of your positive thoughts down, and always reflect on the things you've written, they'll trigger you to your potential.

1. What unique skills, talents, or experiences do I possess that could benefit those around me or contribute to positive change in the world?
2. How can I contribute to causes or organizations that align with my values and make a positive impact on a larger scale?
3. How can I lead by example and inspire others to engage in acts of service and compassion?
4. What steps can I take to collaborate with like-minded individuals or join existing initiatives that aim to create positive change in the world?
5. How can I practice empathy and put myself in others' shoes to better understand their perspectives and needs?

Now, let's continue on the exploration of connecting with others and contributing to the world. But first, let's talk about the incredible power of authentic connection and how it can positively impact your life. When you engage in genuine, heartfelt connections with others, you open the door to a world of enriching experiences and meaningful relationships. You see, when you are your authentic self and show vulnerability, it allows others to do the same. This creates a safe and nurturing environment for both you and those around you to express your true thoughts and feelings. It's in these moments of openness that true connections are forged. When you genuinely listen to others, understanding their perspectives and sharing your own, you create a bond built on trust and empathy. Through authentic connections, you gain a sense of belonging and support. You no longer feel like you have to face life's challenges alone. The power of authentic connection lies in its ability to uplift and inspire you to be your best self. When you surround yourself with people who accept you for who you are, it boosts your confidence and encourages you to embrace your uniqueness. Moreover, authentic connections foster personal growth and self-awareness. As you engage in meaningful conversations, you learn from different perspectives and life experiences. You discover new ideas, interests, and passions that you might not have encountered on your own. These connections become mirrors reflecting the best parts of yourself and revealing areas where you can improve and grow.

Authentic connections are also essential for emotional well-being. When you share your joys, triumphs, fears, and challenges with others, it lightens your emotional burden. It's like having a support system that provides comfort and encouragement during difficult times and celebrates your successes with genuine happiness.

These connections also contribute to your happiness and overall life satisfaction. When you have people you can count on, life feels more fulfilling and meaningful. You find joy in sharing experiences, creating memories, and supporting each other through life's ups and downs. In the professional sphere, authentic connections can lead to exciting opportunities. When you build authentic relationships with colleagues, mentors, or clients, it opens doors for collaboration, mentorship, and career growth. People are more likely to trust and work with someone they feel connected to and who demonstrates integrity and genuineness. Ultimately, the power of authentic connection lies in its ability to create a ripple effect of positive change. When you connect authentically with others, you inspire them to do the same with those they encounter. It's like a chain reaction of kindness, empathy, and understanding, making the world a better place, one genuine connection at a time. Remember, you are worthy of genuine connections, and the world is waiting to embrace the real you.

Henry Ford's early years were marked by curiosity and a keen interest in machinery. He displayed remarkable skills in tinkering and fixing things, learning the intricacies of engines and mechanics at a young age. At sixteen, he left his family's farm to pursue an apprenticeship as a machinist in Detroit, where he honed his craft and further nurtured his passion for all things mechanical. In 1891, Ford found himself working as an engineer for the Edison Illuminating Company. During this time, his fascination with internal combustion engines grew, and he dedicated his spare time to building his first automobile. In 1896, he unveiled his "Quadricycle," a simple gasoline-powered vehicle with four bicycle wheels, that marked the beginning of his automotive journey.

After some initial success with the Quadricycle, Ford founded the Detroit Automobile Company in 1899. Unfortunately, this venture faced financial challenges and closed its doors just two years later. Undeterred by this setback, Ford used the experience to learn from his mistakes and set out on a new path.

In 1903, the Ford Motor Company was born, with a vision to create affordable, reliable automobiles for the masses. Ford believed in democratizing the automobile, making it accessible to the average person rather than a luxury reserved for the wealthy elite. This vision led him to introduce the Model T in 1908, a groundbreaking vehicle that would change the course of automotive history. The Model T, affectionately known as the "Tin Lizzie," was the first mass-produced car, employing innovative assembly line techniques to significantly reduce production time and costs. Ford's revolutionary approach to manufacturing made the Model T affordable for millions of Americans, and it quickly became a symbol of progress and mobility.

As the Ford Motor Company thrived, Henry Ford's impact on the world extended beyond automobiles. In 1914, he introduced the concept of a $5-a-day wage for his workers, nearly doubling their pay. This move was unprecedented at the time and reflected Ford's belief that paying his employees well would create a loyal and motivated workforce. It also set a precedent for the concept of a minimum wage and worker benefits. In addition to his contributions to the automotive industry and labour practices, Ford was also a pioneer in the development of innovative manufacturing processes. He further refined the assembly line approach, leading to increased efficiency and productivity across industries worldwide. However, as time went on, Ford's rigid management style and refusal to innovate led to some challenges for the company. By the late 1920s, the Model T's popularity began to wane as other automakers introduced more advanced models. Realizing the need for change, Ford finally ceased production of the Model T in 1927 and introduced the Model A, a more modern and stylish car that was well-received by the public.

Despite the challenges, Ford's impact on the automotive industry and society at large remained immeasurable. He continued to experiment and innovate throughout his life, making contributions in fields as diverse as agriculture and renewable energy.

On April 7, 1947, Henry Ford passed away at the age of 83, leaving behind a legacy that transcends generations. His vision, tenacity, and commitment to progress revolutionized transportation and manufacturing, forever changing the world and leaving an enduring mark on modern society. Today, Ford's name remains synonymous with innovation, entrepreneurship, and the pioneering spirit. His story serves as a timeless reminder that with perseverance, ingenuity, and a belief in one's dreams, anything is possible. Henry Ford's legacy continues to inspire countless individuals to reach for the stars and make a difference in the world.

Let's talk about empathy and compassion, two powerful qualities that can profoundly impact your relationships and the way you interact with the world. Empathy and compassion go hand in hand, and together, they have the potential to create a more empathetic and caring society. Empathy is the ability to put yourself in someone else's shoes, to understand and share their feelings and experiences. When you practice empathy, you open yourself up to truly connecting with others on a deeper level. You can recognize and validate their emotions, even if you haven't personally experienced the same situation. It's like tuning into their emotional frequency and letting them know, "I see you, I hear you, and I understand what you're going through."

By cultivating empathy, you become more attuned to the needs and struggles of those around you. It allows you to be a source of support and comfort during challenging times, offering a listening ear or a shoulder to lean on. Empathy fosters a sense of belonging and creates an environment where people feel seen and valued, which is essential for building strong, meaningful relationships. In subsequent chapters I'll explore to you the principles of connecting with others and contributing to the world which include:

- **Building Authentic Relationships**
- **Discovering Your Unique Contribution**
- **Making a Positive Impact**

Now, let's talk about compassion. Compassion is the natural outcome of empathy. It's the deep concern and care you feel for someone's well-being when you empathize with their emotions. Compassion moves you to take action, to offer help and assistance, and to be there for others in a meaningful way. When you practice compassion, you extend a helping hand to those who are struggling, experiencing pain, or facing difficulties. It's the warm embrace of kindness and understanding that can brighten someone's darkest moments.

Compassion prompts you to act with love and selflessness, not expecting anything in return, but simply because you want to alleviate someone else's suffering. Together, empathy and compassion create a powerful force for positive change in the world. When you cultivate these qualities, you become an agent of kindness and understanding. You become someone who makes a difference in the lives of others, just by being there for them and showing that you care.

And the beauty of empathy and compassion is that they are not limited to specific situations or people. You can practice empathy and compassion in your personal relationships, at work, in your community, and even with strangers you encounter in your daily life. Each small act of empathy and compassion has the potential to create a ripple effect of kindness and make the world a better place. So, my friend, I encourage you to nurture empathy and compassion within yourself. Take a moment to pause and truly listen to others, seek to understand their feelings, and offer a kind word or gesture whenever you can. Embrace the power of empathy and compassion, and watch how it transforms your relationships and the world around you. Remember, every act of empathy and compassion matters, and together, we can create a more caring and compassionate world.

Now, to the beautiful concept of embracing diversity and how it can enrich your life and the world around you. Embracing diversity means valuing and celebrating the differences that make each person unique and recognizing that these differences contribute to the rich tapestry of humanity. When you embrace diversity, you open yourself up to a world of varied perspectives, cultures, and experiences. Instead of seeing differences as barriers, you begin to see them as bridges that connect you to others in a profound and meaningful way. You become more open-minded and accepting, allowing you to learn from people whose backgrounds and beliefs may be different from your own. By embracing diversity, you cultivate empathy and compassion for others. You begin to understand the challenges and triumphs that people from diverse backgrounds face, and this understanding strengthens your ability to connect with them on a deeper level. Empathy becomes a powerful tool that fosters meaningful relationships and creates a sense of unity in the midst of diversity. Moreover, embracing diversity leads to personal growth and self-awareness. When you expose yourself to different cultures and ways of thinking, you broaden your horizons and challenge your own assumptions and biases. This self-reflection can lead to personal transformation and a greater understanding of your place in the world. Embracing diversity also allows you to become a positive force for change. By championing inclusivity and equality, you create an environment where everyone feels valued and respected. You have the power to stand up against discrimination and prejudice, promoting a world where diversity is not just tolerated but celebrated.

In workplaces and communities, embracing diversity leads to increased creativity and innovation. When people with different backgrounds and perspectives come together, they bring a wealth of ideas and solutions to the table. This collaborative spirit fosters a dynamic and thriving environment that benefits everyone involved.

Let's talk about the incredible power of sharing knowledge and skills, and how doing so can positively impact both your life and the lives of others around you. When you share your knowledge and skills with others, you become a catalyst for growth and empowerment. You see, you have a unique set of knowledge and talents that no one else possesses in quite the same way. By sharing what you know, whether it's academic knowledge, practical skills, or life experiences, you have the ability to inspire and educate others. You become a valuable resource for those seeking to learn and improve themselves.

When you share your knowledge, you not only benefit others but also reinforce your own understanding of the subject matter. Teaching someone else forces you to organize your thoughts and communicate clearly, deepening your grasp of the topic. It's a win-win situation where both you and the recipient gain valuable insights.

Moreover, sharing your skills can create a ripple effect of positive change. When you teach someone a skill, you give them the tools to succeed and thrive. This empowerment can lead to greater opportunities and possibilities for the individual, opening doors they may not have even known existed. As a result, you become a mentor and guide, playing a pivotal role in someone else's personal and professional growth.

Sharing knowledge and skills also fosters a sense of community and connection. When you help someone learn or improve, you create a bond based on mutual respect and support. It's like being part of a team where everyone helps each other succeed, and this camaraderie can lead to lasting and meaningful relationships.

In a broader sense, sharing knowledge and skills contributes to the betterment of society as a whole. When people come together to share their expertise, innovation flourishes, and progress accelerates. It's how we, as a collective, continue to advance and address challenges effectively. You uplift others, create a sense of community, and contribute to the collective growth of humanity.

The acts of kindness are those simple, yet heartfelt gestures that show you care and make a difference in someone's day. They can be as small as offering a warm smile to a stranger or lending a helping hand to someone in need. When you engage in acts of kindness, you spread positivity and compassion to those around you. The beauty of acts of kindness lies in their simplicity. You don't need grand gestures or elaborate plans to make a difference in someone's life. Sometimes, the smallest acts can have the most significant impact. Whether it's offering a listening ear to a friend in distress or surprising a loved one with a thoughtful gift, these acts can brighten someone's day and bring joy to their heart. And here's the remarkable thing about acts of kindness – they have a ripple effect. When you extend kindness to others, it inspires them to do the same for someone else. It creates a chain reaction of positivity, where one act of kindness leads to another and another, creating a wave of goodwill in the world.

Now, let's talk about service. Service goes beyond acts of kindness. It involves dedicating your time, skills, and resources to help others and contribute to the greater good. When you engage in service, you become a force for positive change in your community and beyond. Service can take many forms. It might involve volunteering for a cause you're passionate about, participating in community clean-ups, or supporting a local charity. When you give back to your community, you become an active participant in making the world a better place.

But service isn't just about helping others; it also brings immense fulfillment to your own life. When you see the impact of your actions and the smiles on the faces of those you've helped, it fills your heart with a sense of purpose and joy. Service enriches your life, providing you with a deeper connection to the world and a sense of gratitude for what you have. And here's the best part – you don't need to be a superhero or have endless resources to engage in acts of kindness and service. All it takes is a willingness to show compassion and a desire to make a positive difference. Whether it's a random act of kindness to a stranger or dedicating a few hours of your time to a local cause, your actions matter, and they contribute to a more compassionate and caring world. So, let your kindness shine, and let your service be a beacon of hope and positivity in the world.

Let's dive into the empowering concept of creating positive change and how it can be a driving force for personal growth and making a difference in the world around you. Creating positive change starts with you. It begins with a desire to make things better, whether it's in your own life, your community, or on a global scale. When you take the initiative to create positive change, you become an agent of progress and transformation. The first step in creating positive change is identifying the areas in your life or the world that you want to improve. It could be something as simple as adopting healthier habits or something more significant, like advocating for a cause you deeply care about. Once you've identified your goals, you can start taking action.

Positive change often requires courage and perseverance. It may involve stepping out of your comfort zone, challenging the status quo, and pushing through obstacles. But remember, with determination and belief in yourself, you can overcome any challenges that come your way. Creating positive change is not just about making a grand gesture; it's about embracing everyday opportunities to make a difference. It could be by spreading kindness and compassion through small acts of generosity or by being a source of support for someone in need. These seemingly small actions have the power to create a significant impact.

Moreover, positive change is contagious. When you take the initiative to create positive change in your life, it inspires and motivates others to do the same. Your actions serve as a beacon of hope, encouraging those around you to join you on your journey to make the world a better place. Remember that positive change doesn't happen overnight. It's a gradual process that requires patience and persistence. Celebrate each step you take towards your goals, and don't be disheartened by setbacks. With every effort, you're making progress, and that progress is contributing to a brighter future.

Creating positive change is also about collaboration and community. By connecting with like-minded individuals who share your vision for a better world, you amplify the impact of your efforts. Together, you can create a collective force for positive transformation. Remember, you have the ability to create a ripple effect of positivity that extends far beyond your own life. Be the catalyst for change, and watch as your actions inspire others to do the same.

Let's talk about the importance of nurturing emotional intelligence and how it can positively impact your life and relationships. Emotional intelligence is the ability to understand and manage your own emotions and empathize with the emotions of others. When you nurture your emotional intelligence, you become more in tune with your feelings and reactions. You develop a deeper understanding of what triggers your emotions and how they influence your thoughts and behaviors. By being aware of your emotions, you can respond to situations in a more thoughtful and controlled manner.

Emotional intelligence is like a compass that guides you through life's ups and downs. When you understand your emotions, you become better equipped to handle stress, setbacks, and challenges. Instead of letting your emotions overwhelm you, you can navigate through them with grace and resilience.

Moreover, nurturing emotional intelligence allows you to build stronger and more meaningful relationships. When you can recognize and empathize with the emotions of others, you become a better listener and a more compassionate friend, partner, or colleague. You create a safe space for others to express themselves, fostering deeper connections based on trust and understanding.

Emotional intelligence also plays a vital role in conflict resolution. When you understand your emotions and those of others, it becomes easier to find common ground and work towards resolutions that benefit everyone involved. Instead of reacting impulsively to conflicts, you can approach them with empathy and open communication.

Nurturing emotional intelligence also means being kind and patient with yourself. It's about acknowledging that you're human and that you will experience a range of emotions. Instead of judging yourself for feeling a certain way, you can practice self-compassion and allow yourself to process your emotions in a healthy way.

There are many ways to nurture your emotional intelligence. Engaging in self-reflection, journaling, and mindfulness practices can help you become more aware of your emotions and thoughts. Seeking feedback from others and being open to constructive criticism can also aid in your emotional growth.Remember, nurturing emotional intelligence is a lifelong journey. It's not about being perfect but about making a conscious effort to understand yourself and others better. As you continue to cultivate emotional intelligence, you'll find that it positively impacts every aspect of your life, leading to more fulfilling relationships and greater emotional well-being.

Let's delve into the concept of leaving a lasting legacy and how it can shape the way you live your life and the impact you have on the world. Leaving a lasting legacy is about creating a meaningful and enduring impact that extends far beyond your own lifetime. It's about how you choose to live your life, the values you uphold, and the contributions you make to the world.

You have the power to shape your legacy through the actions you take and the way you treat others. How you interact with people, the kindness and compassion you show, and the positive influence you have on their lives all contribute to the legacy you leave behind.

Leaving a lasting legacy is not about seeking fame or recognition. It's about the genuine desire to make a difference and leave the world a better place. Your legacy is a reflection of your character, your values, and the mark you leave on the hearts of those you touch.

To create a lasting legacy, think about the causes and passions that resonate deeply with you. What issues or values do you want to champion? How can you use your unique talents and strengths to contribute to those causes? You don't have to do something grandiose to leave a lasting legacy. Even the smallest acts of kindness, like helping a neighbor in need or mentoring a younger person, can have a profound impact. It's about the sincerity and genuineness behind your actions that make a lasting impression.

Your legacy is not just about the things you do; it's also about the values you instill in others. The way you lead by example and inspire others to live with purpose and integrity can shape their own legacies. Your positive influence can create a ripple effect of goodness that continues long after you're gone. Leaving a lasting legacy is about living a life that aligns with your deepest values and beliefs. It's about being true to yourself, being kind to others, and making a positive impact in any way you can.

Remember, you have the power to shape your legacy every day through your choices and actions. Embrace the opportunity to make a difference, no matter how big or small, and let your legacy be a testament to the goodness and love you brought into the world. Be mindful of the legacy you want to leave behind, and let your actions reflect the values that matter most to you. Your legacy can be a source of inspiration and comfort to those who follow in your footsteps, making the world a better place for generations to come.

One of the most significant benefits of connecting with others and contributing to the world is by reading quality books, jt is the opportunity to expand your horizons. Whether it's non-fiction books that delve into various subjects, providing valuable insights and knowledge, or fictional stories that transport you to different worlds and perspectives, each book offers a unique journey of exploration and learning. It's not just about reading for the sake of entertainment; it's about immersing yourself in the world of knowledge, wisdom, and imagination that books offer. Quality books are like windows to the minds of the authors, allowing you to tap into their experiences, thoughts, and emotions. By reading such books, you gain access to the accumulated wisdom of others, offering you a chance to broaden your understanding of the human experience and the world we live in. Moreover, reading quality books stimulates your imagination and creativity. As you immerse yourself in a well-crafted story, your mind paints vivid images and scenarios, and you become an active participant in the narrative. This creative engagement can inspire you to think outside the box and see possibilities you might not have considered before.

Once upon a time, there was a passionate book lover named Jenny. From a very young age, Jenny found solace, excitement, and endless possibilities within the pages of books. The love affair with literature started when Jenny was just a child, sitting cross-legged on the floor of the local library, eagerly flipping through picture books, completely captivated by the colourful illustrations and enchanting tales.

As Jenny grew older, the taste in books evolved, and the appetite for knowledge expanded. Novels became Jenny's closest companions, offering adventures in far-off lands, magical encounters, and heartfelt connections with fictional characters that felt like true friends. Each book was an invitation to explore new perspectives, cultures, and time periods, broadening Jenny's understanding of the world. The local bookstore became a second home to Jenny, a place where the smell of ink and paper felt comforting, and the sight of shelves filled with books sparked an immense joy. Jenny couldn't resist running fingers along the spines, contemplating which world to dive into next. In the digital age, e-books and audiobooks became companions on daily commutes and long journeys. Jenny adapted to new formats, embracing technology's convenience while cherishing the essence of the written word. The love for physical books, however, remained unchanged. There was an unexplainable joy in holding a book, feeling the texture of its pages, and leaving handwritten notes in the margins. Over the years, Jenny's reading journey has been filled with laughter, tears, and profound revelations. From classic masterpieces to contemporary bestsellers, each book left an indelible mark on Jenny's heart and mind.
In the end, the story of Jenny and books is an ongoing adventure, an ever-evolving relationship with literature that continues to shape, inspire, and define the essence of who Jenny truly is—a book lover at heart, forever enchanted by the written word.

Reading quality books helps your mental stimulation Reading engages the mind and keeps it active. It improves cognitive functions such as memory, concentration, and critical thinking. Analyzing complex plots or understanding intricate concepts in non-fiction books challenges the brain, promoting mental agility and problem-solving abilities. In summary, reading quality books enriches lives in numerous ways, enhancing knowledge, mental acuity, empathy, and creativity. It opens the door to new experiences and perspectives, ultimately contributing to personal development and a deeper understanding of the world.

In conclusion, by reaching out and engaging with people from different backgrounds, cultures, and experiences, you open up a world of possibilities. Each connection you forge allows you to exchange ideas, learn from one another, and create a positive impact on both a personal and global level. When you genuinely listen to others, empathize with their struggles, and share your own stories, you create a sense of understanding and unity. Through these interactions, you build bridges of compassion and respect, breaking down barriers and fostering a more inclusive society. Your contributions to the world, no matter how small they may seem, are vital. Every act of kindness, support, and assistance that you extend to those in need has a ripple effect. You inspire others to follow your example, creating a chain reaction of positive change. Whether you engage in volunteer work, advocate for meaningful causes, or simply offer a helping hand to a friend, your actions hold the power to uplift individuals and communities. Remember that even the smallest gestures can brighten someone's day and remind them that they are not alone. The impact you have on the world is not limited to your immediate surroundings. Through the interconnectedness of our global community, your actions have the potential to reach far beyond borders, influencing lives you may never even encounter.

I.   Building Authentic Relationships

It was a sunny day in early spring when fate's hand gently guided me towards the love of my life, Katie. I had just moved to a bustling city for a new job, and everything felt fresh and exciting. Little did I know that this new chapter of my life would be forever shaped by a chance encounter that turned into a lifelong love story. On that fateful afternoon, I decided to explore my new neighbourhood, hoping to stumble upon hidden gems and get a feel for the vibrant city life. As I meandered through the streets, I found myself drawn to a cozy café with a welcoming atmosphere. The aroma of freshly brewed coffee and the gentle hum of conversations enticed me to step inside. As I stood in line to order, I couldn't help but notice a woman with a radiant smile and kind eyes standing ahead of me. There was an air of warmth and approachability about her that immediately put me at ease. Her name tag read "Katie," and as fate would have it, she would become the heart and soul of my life. In essence, what I'm trying to express here is that building authentic relationships is all about forming deep, meaningful connections with those around you. It's about being genuine, empathetic, and understanding. In this subtopic, I'm going to share some insights on how you can cultivate authentic relationships that bring joy and fulfillment into your life. You have the power to create lasting bonds, and it all starts with you.

But first let's start from understanding yourself. The foundation of any authentic relationship begins with self-discovery. Before you can truly connect with others, you must first come to know yourself. Reflect on your values, passions, strengths, and vulnerabilities. Embrace the unique essence that defines you, for it is this authentic self that you will share with others in your quest for meaningful connections.

UNDERSTANDING YOURSELF
Absolutely! Understanding yourself is like embarking on a journey of self-discovery, peeling back the layers of who you are and gaining insights into your thoughts, emotions, and values.

Imagine taking some quiet moments to reflect on your thoughts and feelings. You might ask yourself, "What are my passions? What are the things that truly bring me joy and fulfillment?" Understanding yourself begins with acknowledging and embracing your genuine interests and desires, as they are the compass that guides you towards a life of purpose and happiness. Exploring your emotions is another essential part of understanding yourself. You know, it's okay to feel a range of emotions, from happiness and excitement to sadness and frustration. Emotions are like colourful brush strokes that paint the canvas of your experiences. When you allow yourself to feel and acknowledge these emotions, you gain a deeper understanding of what drives you and how you react to different situations.

At the same time, it's okay to acknowledge that you may have areas where you'd like to improve. It's a part of being human. When you embrace your imperfections, you open the door to self-compassion and growth. Every challenge you encounter is an opportunity for learning and becoming a better version of yourself. Understanding yourself also involves being in tune with your values and beliefs. What are the guiding principles that shape your decisions and actions? Reflecting on your values helps you align your life with what truly matters to you, creating a sense of authenticity and purpose.

MAINTAINING BOUNDARIES

Of course! Maintaining boundaries is like drawing a line that defines your personal space and limits, ensuring that you feel respected, safe, and in control of your own well-being. Imagine boundaries as an invisible fence around your emotional and physical space. It's about recognizing what feels comfortable and right for you and communicating that to others. Just like how you'd set a fence around your garden to protect the flowers, maintaining boundaries is about protecting your own peace and happiness. Setting and maintaining boundaries might seem a bit daunting at first, but it's a crucial aspect of building healthy relationships and taking care of yourself. It's like saying, "This is where I stand, and this is what I'm okay with." Boundaries help you maintain your sense of individuality and prevent others from crossing lines that make you uncomfortable or anxious. Let's say you have a friend who tends to be very demanding of your time and energy. Maintaining boundaries in this scenario means expressing your needs and limits kindly but firmly. You might say something like, "I value our friendship, but I also need some time for myself to recharge. I can't always be available, but I'm here for you when I can." By doing so, you show that you care about the relationship while also respecting your own need for space and balance. Boundaries also extend to physical boundaries, like personal space and touch. It's essential to feel comfortable and secure in your physical interactions with others. If someone invades your personal space or makes you uncomfortable with their touch, you have every right to assert your boundaries by stepping back or expressing your discomfort.

When you maintain boundaries, you cultivate a sense of self-respect and self-worth. It shows others that you value yourself and that you expect to be treated with respect and consideration. Healthy boundaries lead to more authentic connections, as people learn to understand and appreciate your limits.

Lastly, don't be afraid to reassess and adjust your boundaries as needed. Life changes, and so do your needs and preferences. Maintaining boundaries is a continuous process of self-awareness and self-care, and it's entirely okay to make adjustments along the way.

REVEL IN IMPERFECTION

Absolutely! "Revel in imperfection" is a beautiful concept that encourages us to embrace our flaws and the imperfections of others, recognizing that they are what make us human and unique. You know, life can sometimes feel like a constant pursuit of perfection – striving to be flawless in everything we do and to have everything around us picture-perfect. But here's the thing: no one is perfect, and that's okay! Revelling in imperfection means celebrating our quirks, mistakes, and the little idiosyncrasies that make us who we are.

Think about it like this: you have this hobby you adore, like playing the guitar or painting. When you first started, you might have hit the wrong chords or created messy brushstrokes, but you didn't give up. You embraced those imperfections as part of your learning journey, and now, your unique style shines through in your creations. You revel in the fact that your art is one-of-a-kind, imperfectly perfect, just like you.

The same goes for the people around you. You've surely noticed how your friends or family have their quirks and little imperfections. But instead of judging or trying to change them, you accept and cherish those aspects, understanding that they are an essential part of who they are. It's like a puzzle, where each piece fits together to create a beautiful and authentic connection.

Revelling in imperfection is liberating because it means we don't have to pretend to be something we're not. It allows us to drop the mask, to let our guard down, and to show our vulnerability. You see, vulnerability isn't a weakness; it's a strength. When we're authentic and genuine, it creates a safe space for others to do the same. It's also about being kinder to ourselves. We all have those days when we feel like we didn't live up to our expectations or made a mistake. But instead of being overly critical, let's treat ourselves with compassion and understanding. We're human, after all – wonderfully imperfect, just like everyone else.

GIVING WITHOUT EXPECTING

Let's talk about the concept of giving without expecting anything in return. Imagine this scenario: You have a close friend who's been going through a tough time lately. They've been feeling overwhelmed with work, family responsibilities, and personal challenges. As their friend, you genuinely care about their well-being and want to support them during this difficult period.

Giving without expecting anything in return means being there for your friend selflessly and without any hidden agenda. You reach out to them, not because you want something in return, but because you genuinely want to offer a listening ear, a helping hand, or a shoulder to lean on.

You call or meet up with your friend, and instead of focusing on your own needs or problems, you make their concerns the priority. You listen attentively, without interrupting or trying to offer immediate solutions. Your genuine presence and empathy allow them to open up and share their feelings without fear of judgement.

During your conversation, you realize that your friend could use some practical help. Without hesitation, you offer your assistance in whatever way you can, whether it's helping with household chores, running errands, or providing a safe space for them to relax and unwind. The beauty of giving without expecting anything in return lies in the purity of your intentions. You're not doing it for recognition or to be repaid in the future. Your sole motivation is to make a positive difference in your friend's life and to show them that they are not alone in their struggles. As days pass, you continue to support your friend through their ups and downs. Sometimes, they may express their gratitude, but you don't seek praise or acknowledgement for your actions. Your fulfillment comes from knowing that you've made a genuine impact and provided comfort during their challenging times.

It's important to note that giving without expectation doesn't mean neglecting your own well-being. It means finding a healthy balance between being there for others and taking care of yourself. When you give selflessly, you do so willingly and with an open heart, knowing that true giving comes from a place of abundance, not scarcity.

FORGIVENESS AND GROWTH

Forgiveness and growth are powerful concepts that go hand in hand, and they have the potential to transform your life in remarkable ways. You know, forgiveness is not about condoning or excusing someone's hurtful actions. It's about releasing the emotional burden that you've been carrying, freeing yourself from the weight of resentment and anger. When you hold onto grudges, it's like carrying a heavy backpack of negative emotions everywhere you go. But forgiveness allows you to drop that load, giving you the freedom to walk with a lighter heart. When you forgive, you give yourself the gift of peace and inner healing. It doesn't mean forgetting what happened or pretending that it didn't hurt. Instead, it's a conscious choice to let go of the pain, making room for growth and new possibilities in your life.

Forgiveness is a process, and it's okay if it takes time. It might start with acknowledging your feelings and accepting that you've been hurt. Then, you can begin to consider the possibility of forgiving the person who hurt you. Remember, forgiveness is not for their sake; it's for yours. By letting go of resentment, you break free from the emotional chains that have been holding you back.

Forgiveness allows you to shift your focus from dwelling on the past to embracing the present and looking towards the future. You become more open to new experiences, relationships, and opportunities. Instead of being defined by the hurtful event, you start defining your own path.

Growth is a continuous journey of self-discovery and self-improvement. It's about learning from your experiences, including the ones that have caused you pain. By forgiving, you gain valuable insights into yourself and others. You develop resilience and emotional maturity, which empowers you to handle challenging situations with grace and wisdom.

As you forgive and grow, you become more compassionate towards yourself and others. You learn to extend forgiveness not just to those who hurt you, but also to yourself for any mistakes or shortcomings. Self-forgiveness is an essential part of the growth process, allowing you to let go of regrets and embrace self-acceptance.

CELEBRATE SMALL MOMENTS

Absolutely! Celebrating small moments is about finding joy and appreciation in the little things that often go unnoticed. It's like collecting sparkling gems scattered throughout your everyday life. Let me explain it in a way that you understand.

Life can sometimes feel like a whirlwind of big events and grand milestones, but there's so much magic in the small moments that deserve celebration too. Imagine this: you wake up on a beautiful morning, and the sun is shining through your window. Instead of rushing through your morning routine, you take a moment to savour the warmth of the sunlight on your face and the peacefulness of the moment. It's a small moment, but it fills your heart with gratitude and sets a positive tone for the day ahead.

You know, we often get caught up in chasing after the next big achievement or milestone, but in doing so, we might overlook the simple joys that surround us. Celebrating small moments means finding delight in the seemingly mundane, like sharing a genuine laugh with a friend, receiving a heartfelt compliment, or even enjoying a delicious cup of coffee.

Think about how wonderful it feels when you receive a thoughtful text message from a loved one, just to say they're thinking of you. It's a small gesture, but it warms your heart and reminds you of the love and connection you share. By celebrating these small gestures, you nurture the bond between you and your loved ones, making your relationships even more meaningful.

Even in challenging times, there are small moments that deserve celebration. Picture this: you've been working hard on a project, and you finally complete a difficult task that's been giving you trouble. It may not be the final accomplishment, but taking a moment to acknowledge your progress and effort can be incredibly empowering and motivating.

LEARNING FROM DIFFERENCES

Learning from differences is like opening a door to a world of diverse perspectives, experiences, and cultures. It's about embracing the beauty of our individual uniqueness and using it as an opportunity to grow, broaden our horizons, and foster understanding.

You know, one of the most incredible things about life is the diversity that surrounds us. Each person we meet, each culture we encounter, and each experience we have brings something unique to the table. Learning from differences means being open-minded and curious about the many ways people navigate through life. Imagine meeting someone from a different cultural background. Instead of approaching them with preconceived notions or judgments, you're genuinely interested in understanding their customs, traditions, and values. You ask questions, listen attentively, and appreciate the richness of their heritage. In doing so, you gain new insights and expand your own perspective on the world.

When you're open to learning from differences, you also cultivate empathy and compassion. You recognize that everyone has their own struggles and triumphs, and you're willing to walk in their shoes for a moment to understand their journey. This understanding creates bonds of connection and breaks down barriers that might otherwise separate us.

Differences don't have to divide us; they can be bridges that connect us to one another. You know, it's like discovering a treasure trove of wisdom hidden within the hearts of those around you. Each person you encounter has a story to share, lessons to impart, and a unique perspective on life.

Learning from differences doesn't mean you have to abandon your own beliefs or values. Instead, it's about finding common ground and embracing the tapestry of diversity that weaves us all together. Like a beautiful symphony with various instruments, we harmonize and create a richer, more vibrant melody when we celebrate our differences.

HONESTY AND TRANSPARENCY

Honesty and transparency are like the pillars that hold the foundation of trust and authenticity in any relationship. You know, honesty and transparency are the cornerstones of building genuine and meaningful connections with others. They're like a clear window that allows people to see your true self without any hidden agendas or pretences. When you're honest and transparent, you create an atmosphere of openness and trust that strengthens your relationships.

Let's say you're having a conversation with a close friend, and they ask you for your opinion on a matter that's important to them. Instead of sugarcoating your response or telling them what you think they want to hear, you choose to be honest. You share your genuine thoughts and feelings, even if it means having a difficult conversation. Being honest doesn't mean being harsh or hurtful; it means expressing yourself with kindness and integrity. Your friend might appreciate your honesty because they know they can rely on you to give them sincere feedback. In this way, honesty becomes the bedrock of a strong and authentic friendship.

Transparency is like being an open book, allowing others to see your intentions, actions, and emotions. When you're transparent, you don't hide behind a facade or keep secrets. Instead, you're upfront and genuine in your interactions with others. Let's say you're working on a team project at work. Instead of hiding your progress or ideas, you openly share your thoughts with your colleagues. You communicate your challenges and successes, making it easier for everyone to work together towards a common goal. This transparency fosters a sense of trust within the team, and it encourages open communication and collaboration. Being honest and transparent also means owning up to your mistakes and taking responsibility for your actions. It's about being accountable for your choices and showing that you're willing to learn and grow from them. When you make a mistake, admitting it and being transparent about it can actually strengthen the bond with others, as it shows that you value the truth and are committed to self-improvement.

In conclusion, building authentic relationships is an art that requires intention, effort, and genuine care. It's about nurturing connections that are based on openness, trust, and mutual respect. Throughout this journey, we have explored various key elements that contribute to the beauty and depth of authentic relationships. Empowering each other, celebrating small moments, and learning from differences enrich the tapestry of our connections, allowing us to grow and evolve together. Maintaining healthy boundaries, practicing forgiveness and growth, and giving without expecting anything in return create an atmosphere of understanding and compassion.
Honesty and transparency serve as the foundation of authenticity, fostering an environment where individuals can be their true selves without fear of judgement. By revelling in imperfection, we embrace vulnerability and show compassion for ourselves and others.
In the pursuit of authentic relationships, we find the courage to be honest, to listen actively, and to appreciate the diverse perspectives and experiences that others bring into our lives. Through these connections, we learn, we inspire, and we build bridges of empathy and understanding. Remember, authentic relationships are not perfect, but they are genuine and resilient. They weather the storms and celebrate the joys of life together. As we continue to cultivate these connections, we find that our lives become richer, more meaningful, and filled with love.

II.   Discovering Your Unique Contribution

Discovering one's unique contribution is an extraordinary journey that each of us must embark upon at some point in our lives. It's a path of introspection and self-exploration, where you delve into the depths of your being to uncover the essence of what makes you truly special. This quest is not about comparing yourself to others; rather, it's about celebrating your individuality and the invaluable gifts you possess. As you set foot on this path, the first step is to recognize your passions. What sets your heart ablaze? What activities make you lose track of time? These are the pursuits that fuel your enthusiasm and bring joy to your soul. Embrace them wholeheartedly, for within these passions lies a key to unlocking your unique contribution.
Next, take a moment to appreciate your innate talents. We all have natural abilities that come effortlessly to us. These gifts are like treasures waiting to be unearthed. Embrace them with gratitude and see how they can serve as the building blocks of your unique

contribution. Your talents are not just random skills; they are the essence of what makes you exceptional.

Life experiences, both challenging and uplifting, shape our perspectives and provide valuable insights. Reflect on the journey you've travelled so far, the hurdles you've overcome, and the lessons you've learned. These experiences have sculpted you into the person you are today and hold the potential to add depth and authenticity to your unique contribution.

As you explore your inner self, ponder upon your core values – those guiding principles that define your character. Your core values are the compass that keeps you anchored in times of uncertainty. Aligning your contribution with these values ensures that your impact on the world will be true to who you are at your core.

In this pursuit, do not fear taking risks or experiencing failures. Great achievements often arise from stepping outside of your comfort zone and learning from your setbacks. Embrace failure as an essential part of growth, for it reveals the lessons needed to refine your unique contribution. With your vision in mind, imagine the impact you want to have on the world.

See how your talents, passions, and experiences come together in harmony, weaving a tapestry of positive change. This vision will be your guiding light through moments of doubt and uncertainty.

Seeking feedback from those who know you well can be a valuable part of this voyage. They may see strengths in you that you might have overlooked or underestimated. Listen to their perspectives with an open heart, for they can offer fresh insights that will aid you in honing your contribution.

Life's experiences are the brushstrokes that paint the canvas of your journey. Reflect upon the highs and lows, the challenges and triumphs, for they hold the wisdom that enriches your soul. Your experiences add depth and authenticity to the masterpiece of your unique contribution.

Let your core values be your guiding light, illuminating the path ahead. They are the inner compass that keeps you true to yourself, even amidst the swirling winds of change. Align your contribution with these values, for they are the foundation of your impact on the world.

In this journey, remember that comparison is the thief of joy. Embrace the beauty of your individuality, for you are a marvel unlike any other. Your contribution will be a symphony of uniqueness, and its song shall resonate in harmony with the universe.

Envision the impact you wish to have on the world, for it is the beacon that guides your steps. Let this vision be your north star, leading you through the darkness of uncertainty towards the horizon of your purpose.

In conclusion, may you walk this path with an open heart, unearthing the gems that make you extraordinary. Embrace vulnerability, for it is the gateway to authentic connection. Trust in the journey, for it is yours to explore and cherish. And as you discover your unique contribution, may it shine brightly, illuminating not only your path but also the lives of those you touch.

III. Making a Positive Impact

Making a positive impact is all about leaving a meaningful and lasting mark on the world, contributing to the betterment of society, and creating a ripple effect that can inspire others to do the same. It's about understanding that even the smallest actions can have a significant impact and recognizing the power we have to influence the lives of others and the planet as a whole. To make a positive impact, we must start with ourselves. Self-awareness and personal growth are essential in this journey. Taking the time to reflect on our values, strengths, and weaknesses helps us identify areas where we can make a difference. Setting clear intentions and goals allows us to align our actions with our values, ensuring that we move in the direction of positive change.

Once we've gained self-awareness, it's time to extend that impact to others. Positive impact often begins at the grassroots level, within our local communities. It could involve volunteering for a cause close to our hearts, supporting local businesses, or helping our neighbours in times of need. Small acts of kindness and compassion can have a domino effect, spreading positivity to those around us.

Being environmentally conscious is another crucial aspect of making a positive impact. Taking responsibility for our ecological footprint and adopting sustainable practices can contribute to a healthier planet. Whether it's reducing waste, conserving energy, or supporting eco-friendly initiatives, every effort counts towards creating a more sustainable world for future generations.

Education is a powerful tool in making a positive impact. Sharing knowledge and empowering others with education can break the cycle of poverty and inequality. We can mentor, tutor, or support educational programs that provide opportunities for those less fortunate. When we invest in education, we invest in a brighter future for individuals and the entire community.

Promoting inclusivity and diversity is equally vital. Embracing differences and treating everyone with respect fosters a sense of belonging and unity. By challenging stereotypes and advocating for equal rights, we create a more tolerant and harmonious society where everyone has an equal chance to thrive.

Supporting charitable organizations and social causes can have a far-reaching impact. Donating to reputable nonprofits or participating in fundraising events can aid in addressing pressing issues like hunger, homelessness, healthcare, and more. These contributions combine with others, pooling resources to make a significant difference in the lives of those in need.

In a rapidly evolving world, technology plays an ever-increasing role in making a positive impact. Leveraging technology for social good can amplify our efforts. From online crowdfunding campaigns to using social media to spread awareness about critical issues, technology connects people and resources, making collective action more accessible than ever. As we aim to make a positive impact, it's crucial to practice empathy and active listening. Understanding the needs and concerns of others helps tailor our efforts effectively. Being open to feedback and learning from failures allows us to refine our approach, ensuring that we continuously improve and remain adaptable in an ever-changing world.

In conclusion, making a positive impact is a journey that starts from within and radiates outward. It involves self-awareness, compassion, and a commitment to being a force for good in the world. By taking action in our local communities, caring for the environment, promoting education and inclusivity, supporting charitable causes, leveraging technology, and practicing empathy, we can collectively create a brighter, more equitable future for generations to come. Remember, no effort is too small, as each act of kindness and positive change can spark a chain reaction, making the world a better place one step at a time.

CHAPTER SEVEN

Resilience and the Pursuit of Purpose

"You are the author of your story. Write it with passion and purpose."

Along this path, you will encounter both challenges and opportunities that will test your resilience and lead you toward your ultimate purpose. In this chapter, we'll talk about the exploration of resilience and the pursuit of purpose, I will guide you through the principles of finding your purpose in difficult times, and the reason why you should never give up on any challenges you encounter on you're journey of self-discovery, whilst also I'll take you to the deep insights, advice, and encouragement to help you find the strength within yourself to overcome obstacles and live a purposeful life. One may ask how do I typically respond to challenges and setbacks in my life? What self-limiting beliefs or negative thought patterns hinder my resilience, and how can I work to change them? Do I feel a sense of purpose in my daily life, or do I yearn for a greater sense of direction and meaning? These questions you should ask yourself in your daily life, why these questions are important is that they awaken your inner insight of who you are and how you respond to setbacks and obstacles. Now let me take you to the principles of resilience and the pursuit of purpose.

In the exploration of resilience and the pursuit of purpose, I have engaged in profound self-reflection and introspection. I have come to recognize that resilience is the cornerstone of my inner strength, empowering me to confront challenges head-on and embrace setbacks as opportunities for growth. I acknowledge that my response to adversity shapes my ability to persevere on the path of purpose. I have delved into my passions, values, and interests, discovering the activities that fill me with joy and fulfillment. These reflections have helped me align my goals with my purpose, creating a sense of direction and meaning in my endeavours. I have also recognized the significance of surrounding myself with a supportive network that encourages and uplifts me during difficult times.

Throughout my journey of becoming an author, I have encountered setbacks and faced moments of uncertainty. However, I have come to appreciate these experiences as powerful teachers, providing invaluable lessons that have refined my pursuit of purpose. My willingness to embrace change and adaptability has empowered me to explore new avenues, even when they deviate from my original path. I have learned to celebrate my achievements and progress, no matter how small, as each step brings me closer to realizing my purpose. Moreover, I have cultivated a growth mindset, recognizing that my abilities are not fixed, but rather can be developed through dedication and effort.

In this pursuit, I have discovered the transformative power of self-compassion. I now treat myself with kindness and understanding, acknowledging that setbacks and failures do not define my worth or potential. I have learned to silence self-limiting beliefs and negative thought patterns, nurturing a positive mindset that guides me forward.

Here are five Principles of Resilience and the Pursuit of Purpose:

1. SETTING GOALS WITH PURPOSE

Setting goals with purpose is a powerful way for you to navigate your life with clarity and intention. When you establish goals that are aligned with your purpose, you create a roadmap that leads you towards the life you envision. It's like having a compass that guides you in the right direction, helping you stay focused and motivated along the way. First, take the time to reflect on what truly matters to you. What are your passions, values, and long-term aspirations? This introspection will help you identify your purpose, the driving force that gives meaning to your journey. Your purpose could be anything from pursuing a fulfilling career, making a positive impact on others, or achieving personal growth and happiness. Once you have a clear sense of your purpose, break it down into specific, measurable, attainable, relevant, and time-bound SMART goals. These goals should be like stepping stones that lead you closer to your purpose. For example, if your purpose is to become a successful writer, your SMART goal could be to complete writing a book within the next year. Setting goals with purpose means ensuring that they are meaningful to you and align with your values. It's not about setting goals based on societal expectations or what others want for you. Your goals should resonate deeply with your inner desires and aspirations.

Moreover, remember that your goals are not set in stone. Life is dynamic, and as you grow and evolve, your goals may shift too. Embrace this flexibility and allow yourself to adjust your goals if needed. The key is to stay true to your purpose and make sure your goals continue to reflect what truly matters to you.

As you work towards your goals with purpose, celebrate every milestone and progress you make along the way. Recognize that each step, no matter how small, brings you closer to your purpose. Celebrating your achievements will boost your motivation and reinforce your commitment to the journey. Lastly, don't be discouraged by challenges or setbacks that may arise on your path. Setting goals with purpose doesn't mean it will always be smooth sailing. In fact, challenges can be opportunities for growth and learning. Embrace these obstacles as part of the process and keep pushing forward with resilience and determination.

In summary, setting goals with purpose empowers you to create a fulfilling and intentional life. By aligning your goals with your purpose, you establish a clear direction, stay motivated, and navigate through life with a sense of meaning and fulfillment. So, take the time to discover your purpose, set SMART goals, embrace flexibility, celebrate your progress, and face challenges with resilience as you embark on this purpose-driven journey.

2. LEARNING FROM ROLE MODELS

Learning from role models is an invaluable way for you to gain inspiration, guidance, and wisdom on your own journey. When you look up to someone as a role model, you can observe their actions, experiences, and achievements to understand how they navigated challenges and achieved success. It's like having a mentor by your side, guiding you with their example and showing you what's possible. First, think about the qualities and accomplishments that resonate with you as a role model. What is it about them that you admire? It could be their determination, resilience, leadership skills, or how they make a positive impact on others. Identifying these traits will help you focus on the aspects you want to emulate in your own life.

Once you have your role model in mind, study their journey. Read about their life, watch interviews or documentaries, and listen to their advice. Pay attention to the challenges they faced and how they overcame them. You can learn valuable lessons from their experiences and apply them to your own path.

Remember that you don't have to mimic your role model exactly. Instead, adapt their wisdom to fit your unique circumstances and aspirations. Use their success stories as sources of inspiration and motivation to pursue your own dreams with determination and passion.

Additionally, don't limit yourself to just one role model. You can learn from multiple individuals who have excelled in different aspects of life. Look for role models in various areas, such as career, personal development, relationships, or hobbies. Each role model can provide you with unique insights and perspectives. Learning from role models is not about trying to be exactly like them. It's about identifying the qualities and strategies that resonate with you and incorporating them into your own journey. Use their success stories to fuel your determination and belief in your own potential.

Moreover, don't be discouraged if you encounter challenges that your role models didn't face. Everyone's journey is unique, and you will have your own set of obstacles to overcome. The key is to adapt the lessons you've learned and apply them in ways that best suit your situation.

3. FINDING MEANING IN ADVERSITY

Finding meaning in adversity is a profound and transformative process that can empower you to grow and thrive even in the face of challenges. When you encounter difficult times, you have the power to extract valuable lessons and insights from those experiences, ultimately using them to shape your perspective and actions. During moments of adversity, you might feel overwhelmed or discouraged. It's completely normal to have these emotions. However, remember that you have the strength within you to rise above these challenges. Take a deep breath and remind yourself that you are capable of finding meaning even in the darkest of times. One way to find meaning in adversity is by reflecting on the lessons you've learned and the personal growth you've experienced throughout the journey. Ask yourself what you have discovered about your strengths, resilience, and ability to overcome obstacles. Each challenge you face presents an opportunity for you to discover new aspects of yourself and develop a deeper understanding of your capabilities.

You can also find meaning in adversity by looking for silver linings or positive aspects within the difficult situation. Reflect on the ways in which adversity has pushed you to explore new opportunities, forced you to step outside your comfort zone, or enabled you to reevaluate your priorities. Sometimes, adversity can lead you to unexpected paths or open doors that you didn't realize were there. Moreover, consider how the adversity you've experienced can be a source of inspiration or support for others facing similar struggles. Your journey through adversity can become a beacon of hope and encouragement for those who may be going through similar challenges. Sharing your story and the lessons you've learned can create meaningful connections and provide a sense of purpose in helping others.

While finding meaning in adversity can be a powerful process, it's important to acknowledge that it may take time. Allow yourself to feel the emotions that arise and give yourself the space to process and reflect on the experience. Don't rush the journey; be patient and gentle with yourself as you uncover the meaning within the adversity. Remember, you have the ability to transform hardships into stepping stones for growth and purpose. Embrace the challenges you face, learn from them, and use the lessons to navigate your journey with resilience and a renewed sense of purpose. You are capable of finding meaning in adversity, and as you do, you will emerge stronger, wiser, and more empowered to face whatever life throws your way.

4. EMBODYING RESILIENCE IN DAILY HABITS

Embodying resilience in your daily habits is a powerful way for you to cultivate inner strength and navigate life's challenges with grace and determination. Resilience is not just a trait; it's a skill that you can develop and integrate into your everyday life, empowering you to bounce back from setbacks and approach difficulties with a positive mindset. One of the key ways you can embody resilience in your daily habits is by practicing self-care. Take care of yourself physically, mentally, and emotionally. Prioritize regular exercise, nourishing meals, and sufficient rest to ensure that you have the energy and vitality to face whatever comes your way.

In addition to physical self-care, cultivate habits that nourish your mental and emotional well-being. Practice mindfulness and meditation to stay centred and focused. Engage in activities that bring you joy and reduce stress, such as spending time in nature, reading, or pursuing hobbies. Another essential habit in embodying resilience is cultivating a growth mindset. Remind yourself that setbacks and failures are not indications of your worth or abilities. Instead, view them as opportunities for learning and growth. Embrace challenges with a positive attitude, recognizing that you have the capacity to overcome them and become stronger as a result. Consistency is key in embodying resilience. Establish a daily routine that supports your well-being and goals. Consistently practicing self-care, maintaining a growth mindset, and engaging in activities that promote resilience will reinforce these habits and make them an integral part of your life.

When facing challenges, resist the temptation to avoid or ignore them. Embrace them with courage and take small, manageable steps to tackle them. Break big tasks into smaller ones and celebrate each step you take toward overcoming obstacles. This approach will build your confidence and reinforce your resilience in facing future challenges.

Surround yourself with a supportive network of friends, family, or mentors who uplift and encourage you. Share your experiences and challenges with them, and allow their guidance and encouragement to fuel your resilience. Lastly, be kind and compassionate to yourself throughout the process. Embodying resilience doesn't mean you won't face difficulties, but it means that you approach them with self-compassion and a belief in your ability to rise above them.

In summary, embodying resilience in your daily habits empowers you to thrive in the face of adversity. By practicing self-care, cultivating a growth mindset, staying consistent, and seeking support, you can navigate life's challenges with resilience and grace. Remember, resilience is not something you're born with; it's a skill you can develop and nurture, and it will serve as a powerful asset in shaping the life you desire.

5. THE PURSUIT OF PURPOSE

The pursuit of purpose is a deeply personal and fulfilling journey that is uniquely yours to explore. It's about discovering what truly ignites your passion, aligning your actions with your values, and creating a life that brings you joy and fulfillment. You are the protagonist of this quest, and the choices you make will shape the path you tread. First, take the time to explore your interests, passions, and aspirations. What activities light a fire within you? What causes or issues do you care deeply about? Reflect on what makes you feel alive and connected to the world around you. This self-discovery process is essential in uncovering your purpose and gaining clarity on the direction you want to take. As you embark on this journey, be open to exploring different avenues and possibilities. Your purpose may evolve over time, and that's okay. Embrace the journey of self-discovery, knowing that each experience contributes to shaping your unique path. Setting goals is an important aspect of pursuing your purpose. Define specific, meaningful, and achievable goals that align with your purpose. These goals will serve as guideposts, helping you stay focused and motivated as you move forward.

Remember that the pursuit of purpose is not always a linear path. You may encounter challenges and obstacles along the way. Embrace these moments as opportunities for growth and learning. Your resilience and determination will be your allies in navigating through tough times.

Surround yourself with supportive individuals who believe in you and your purpose. Share your dreams and aspirations with those who uplift and encourage you. Having a supportive network will provide you with the encouragement and inspiration needed to keep going, especially during challenging times.

Be kind to yourself during this journey. Celebrate your progress and acknowledge your achievements, no matter how small. Self-compassion is a powerful tool that will sustain you during moments of self-doubt or setbacks. Stay open to the unexpected opportunities that may present themselves. Sometimes, life may lead you down a path you never envisioned, but it might be the very one that brings you closer to your purpose.

Finally, trust yourself and your intuition. The pursuit of purpose is a deeply personal endeavour, and only you can truly know what brings you fulfillment and meaning. Embrace the journey with an open heart and a willingness to embrace the unknown. In conclusion, the pursuit of purpose is a transformative and enriching journey that allows you to create a life that is meaningful and fulfilling. Trust in yourself, follow your passion, and stay committed to your goals. You have the power to shape your destiny, and as you embark on this path, know that the pursuit of purpose is a testament to the extraordinary potential that resides within you.

I.   Navigating Setbacks and Obstacles

Once upon a time, in a quaint little town, lived a determined young woman named Katie. Her heart was set on a typewriting career, and she knew deep within her soul that this was her purpose in life. Armed with unwavering passion and an indomitable spirit, Katie embarked on a journey of resilience to make her dreams a reality. Katie's fascination with typewriters began during her childhood when she stumbled upon an old, dusty typewriter in her grandparents' attic. The rhythmic sound of the keys and the tangible result of the printed words enchanted her. From that moment, she knew she wanted to create magic with those keys and carve her path as a typist.

In pursuit of her dream, Katie faced naysayers who questioned the relevance of typewriters in the modern age of technology. Undeterred, she viewed these challenges as opportunities to prove her worth and the timeless artistry of typewriting. Katie encountered setbacks along her journey, competing against skilled typists and facing numerous rejections from potential employers. However, with each rejection, her resilience grew stronger. She refused to be discouraged and persevered with the belief that her passion for typewriting would eventually lead her to her rightful place.

During her quest, Katie sought guidance from seasoned typists and mentors who had navigated similar paths in the past. Their wisdom and encouragement fueled her determination, reminding her that she was not alone in her pursuit.

The turning point in Katie's journey came when she stumbled upon an old typewriting competition. It was a chance to showcase her skills and prove the significance of this timeless craft. With renewed vigour, she poured her heart and soul into her performance, leaving the judges spellbound with her precision and artistry. Through her resilience and unwavering determination, Katie achieved her dream of becoming a professional typist. Her typewriting journey not only shaped her career but also touched the lives of countless people who marvelled at her craft.

However, life's journey is a winding road, and along the way, we encounter setbacks and obstacles that can test our mettle. But, fear not, for you possess the strength to face these challenges head-on and emerge even stronger. Let us embark on this empowering journey together, discovering practical strategies and cultivating a positive mindset that will help you conquer life's hurdles with confidence. When life throws a curveball your way, remember that setbacks do not define you. You are more than capable of embracing resilience as your most potent weapon. Embrace challenges as opportunities to grow and learn. Nurture a growth mindset that views obstacles as stepping stones to success. Rise to the occasion with determination and courage, and you'll find that no challenge can hold you back. When facing obstacles, tap into your innate problem-solving skills. Assess the situation calmly and explore various solutions. Seek advice and support from friends, family, or mentors, for a fresh perspective can illuminate the way. You are not alone in this endeavour, and together, we can find the best route forward. Amidst the trials and tribulations, remember to be kind to yourself. Self-compassion is not a sign of weakness but a source of strength. Understand that setbacks are part of being human and that no one is immune to them. Treat yourself as you would a dear friend – with kindness, patience, and understanding.
Every setback carries valuable lessons. Take time to reflect on the experience, extracting wisdom from every trial. Let these lessons become the foundation of your growth and personal development. With a growth-oriented mindset, setbacks transform into stepping stones on your path to success.
As you navigate life's challenges, seek support from those who care about your journey. You are not alone; a helping hand can guide you through the darkest hours. Remember, asking for help is a sign of courage, not weakness. At the core of navigating setbacks and overcoming obstacles lies the most powerful key of all: self-belief. Your belief in yourself can be the driving force that propels you forward, even in the face of seemingly insurmountable challenges. When you truly believe in your abilities and potential, you unlock a reservoir of strength and resilience that can carry you through the toughest of times. Self-belief is not merely a blind confidence; it is an unwavering trust in your capacity to learn, adapt, and grow. With self-belief, you recognize that setbacks are natural parts of the journey and that failure is not a permanent state but a stepping stone toward success.
Embracing self-belief involves silencing the inner critic and cultivating a positive and empowering inner dialogue. Celebrate your achievements, no matter how small, and acknowledge your progress on this winding path. Treat yourself with the same kindness and compassion you would offer a friend facing difficulties.
When you truly believe in yourself, you approach challenges with a proactive attitude. Instead of succumbing to fear or doubt, you confront obstacles with a determination to find solutions and learn from the experience. Self-belief allows you to tap into your problem-solving skills, seek help when needed, and remain adaptable in the face of uncertainty.

Moreover, self-belief fuels perseverance. It grants you the courage to push through setbacks, to rise from failures, and to keep moving forward when others might give up. This unwavering faith in yourself is a beacon of light that shines through the darkest moments, guiding you toward the realization of your dreams.

Nurturing self-belief is a lifelong journey that requires practice and self-awareness. Surround yourself with supportive individuals who believe in your potential and uplift you when doubts arise. Continuously challenge yourself and step outside of your comfort zone, for each accomplishment reinforces your belief in what you can achieve.

Remember, you possess a unique combination of strengths, talents, and experiences that make you capable of facing any challenge that comes your way. Embrace your uniqueness and let self-belief be the driving force behind your pursuit of success and personal growth. In conclusion, self-belief is the most crucial key in navigating setbacks and obstacles. It empowers you to face challenges with resilience, determination, and a growth mindset. Cultivate this powerful belief in yourself, and you will unlock the potential to conquer life's hurdles, realizing that you are truly capable of achieving greatness. Believe in yourself, and the world will believe in you too.

II.   Building Resilience in the Face of Adversity

Adversity, an inevitable companion in the journey of life, presents itself in various forms and at unexpected times. It manifests as challenges, obstacles, or setbacks that test our strength, resilience, and character. While it can be daunting and uncomfortable, adversity is not an enemy to be feared but rather a profound teacher that offers invaluable lessons and opportunities for growth. In its essence, adversity is a powerful catalyst for change and self-discovery. It has the unique ability to reveal the depths of our inner strength, resourcefulness, and determination. When confronted with adversity, we are often pushed beyond our comfort zones, forcing us to confront our fears and insecurities. It is in these moments of discomfort and vulnerability that we find the true essence of who we are. Adversity teaches us the art of resilience—the ability to bounce back from life's trials and emerge stronger than before. Resilience is not a fixed trait but a skill that can be cultivated and honed through facing challenges head-on. Like a muscle that grows stronger with each workout, resilience is developed by navigating through adversity, learning from our experiences, and adapting to changing circumstances. Now let's discuss how we can build resilience in the face of adversity.

Building resilience in the face of adversity is a crucial skill that can transform how you navigate life's challenges. Adversity is an inevitable part of the human experience, and none of us are exempt from its grasp. However, by developing resilience, you can face these challenges head-on with the courage and determination needed to overcome them. When life throws unexpected curveballs your way, the first step towards building resilience is accepting the reality of the situation. It's normal to feel overwhelmed, vulnerable, or even frightened during tough times. Instead of pushing these feelings aside, embrace them. Treat yourself with the same kindness and understanding you would offer a close friend facing a difficult situation. Acknowledge that it's alright to make mistakes and remember that failure can pave the way for growth and valuable learning experiences.

Remember, you don't have to go through tough times alone. Cultivate a strong support system by nurturing meaningful connections with family, friends, and colleagues. Surround yourself with individuals who lift you up and inspire you. Reach out to your loved ones when you need to talk or seek advice. Having a supportive network can provide the emotional support necessary to endure challenging times.

When confronted with adversity, adopt a problem-solving mindset. Rather than being overwhelmed by the magnitude of the problems, break them down into manageable tasks. Create a step-by-step plan to tackle each aspect, and as you accomplish each task, you'll gain the confidence and momentum needed to face the next challenge.

Your mindset plays a vital role in how you handle adversity. Cultivate a positive outlook and focus on the possibilities rather than dwelling on limitations. Recognize and challenge negative thought patterns that can hinder your resilience. Replace negative self-talk with positive affirmations to reinforce your belief in yourself and your abilities.

Reflect on past adversities you've faced and the strategies you employed to overcome them. Identify patterns and successful coping mechanisms that you can apply in current challenges. Recognize that you have overcome difficulties before, and you possess the strength to do so again. Draw upon your past experiences as a source of inspiration and motivation.

During challenging times, set realistic and achievable goals. Break down long-term objectives into smaller milestones, and celebrate each accomplishment along the way. This approach provides a sense of progress, even in the face of adversity, and keeps you focused on moving forward.

In conclusion, building resilience is an ongoing process that requires patience, self-compassion, and determination. It's about facing adversity head-on and growing through life's difficulties. By accepting adversity as a part of life, cultivating a supportive network, developing problem-solving skills, maintaining a positive mindset, practicing mindfulness, learning from past experiences, setting realistic goals, and embracing adaptability, you can strengthen your resilience and navigate life's challenges with greater confidence. Remember, resilience is not about avoiding adversity but rather about growing and thriving in the face of it. With these strategies, you can build resilience that will serve you well throughout your journey in life.

III.   Persevering on the Path of Purpose

Life's journey can be an unpredictable rollercoaster, filled with ups and downs, twists and turns. But amidst this whirlwind, there's something magical that awaits you - your path of purpose. Picture it as a road less travelled, a unique journey that is yours and yours alone. It's that meaningful pursuit that ignites your soul and makes you feel alive. However, the road to purpose is not always smooth sailing, and that's where perseverance becomes your faithful companion.

You see, "purpose" is more than just a buzzword. It's the driving force that gives your life direction and significance. It's the profound answer to the question of why you're here and what you're meant to do. Discovering and embracing your purpose requires self-reflection, soul-searching, and sometimes, a leap of faith. Once you catch a glimpse of that purposeful path, you'll feel an undeniable pull, like a beacon guiding you forward.

As you set forth on this journey, you'll encounter challenges that may seem insurmountable. Doubts will creep in, and obstacles will attempt to block your way. But remember, it's all part of the process. Embrace these moments of struggle as opportunities for growth, and let perseverance light your way. Let's delve into the important steps for persevering on the path of purpose.

FINDING YOUR NORTH STAR:

The first step in persevering on the path of purpose is discovering what truly sets your soul on fire. You might ask yourself, "What makes me come alive? What brings me joy and fulfillment?" You are the architect of your purpose, and the answers to these questions are the bricks that build your dreams. Discovering your North Star begins with introspection and self-awareness. You must look within yourself, exploring your passions, talents, and dreams. Ask yourself what truly sets your soul on fire, what activities make you lose track of time, and what brings you a deep sense of joy and fulfillment. This self-discovery process is all about recognizing the things that make you feel most alive and connected to your purpose.
Be patient with yourself during this journey of self-exploration. Sometimes, it takes time and experience to unearth your North Star. Embrace the process, knowing that each step you take is bringing you closer to that guiding light.
Now, imagine you're standing in the middle of a vast, starry night sky. Among the countless stars that twinkle above, one shines brighter and more intensely than the rest - that's your North Star. It represents your unique calling, the path that's meant for you and you alone. When you begin to identify your North Star, you'll feel an undeniable pull, a sense of excitement and clarity that propels you forward. It's like finding the compass that always points you in the right direction. Trust that feeling, for it is a sign that you're on the right path. In times of uncertainty or when you feel lost, look to your North Star for guidance. It will always be there, shining brightly, ready to steer you in the right direction. Trust yourself and the path you're on, for you have the power to create a life that aligns with your true purpose. But remember, finding your North Star isn't about reaching a fixed destination. It's a continuous journey of growth and self-discovery. As you evolve, your purpose may also evolve, and that's perfectly okay. Embrace the changes, and let your North Star be your constant companion, guiding you through the ebb and flow of life.

EMBRACING FAILURE AS GROWTH:

In the pursuit of purpose, you'll undoubtedly encounter failure at some point. Instead of seeing failure as a dead-end, view it as a stepping stone towards growth. Failure is a natural part of the process, and every successful individual has experienced it. Embrace failure as an opportunity to learn, adapt, and improve. Remember, it's not about how many times you fall, but how many times you rise again.
However, when you experience failure, take a moment to pause and reflect on the experience. Ask yourself, "What can I learn from this situation?" and "How can I use this as a chance to become better?" By doing so, you shift your perspective from dwelling on the disappointment to focusing on the valuable lessons you can extract from the experience. You see, when you encounter failure, it's essential not to see it as a reflection of your worth or capabilities. Instead, view it as an opportunity for growth and self-improvement. Embracing failure means understanding that it's okay to stumble because that's how you learn and evolve.

In these moments, be gentle with yourself. Avoid being overly critical or judgmental. Remember that everyone faces setbacks, and it's okay to feel disappointed or upset. Acknowledge your emotions, but also recognize that failure is just a temporary setback. It doesn't define you or your potential for success. You have the power to turn failure into a catalyst for growth. When you encounter obstacles or make mistakes, take the time to analyze what went wrong and why. This introspection allows you to identify areas where you can improve and make better choices in the future.

Furthermore, don't be afraid to seek feedback from others. Sometimes, an outside perspective can offer valuable insights that you might not have seen on your own. Embrace constructive criticism as a tool for self-improvement, not as a reflection of your inadequacy. Remember, the most successful individuals in history have faced failure, sometimes repeatedly, but they didn't let it deter them from their dreams. Instead, they used failure as motivation to keep pushing forward and striving for greatness. You have the power to turn every setback into a chance for growth and learning. Embrace failure as a natural part of your path, and know that with each failure, you become more resilient, more knowledgeable, and more equipped to take on whatever challenges life may bring your way. Keep your head held high, and never forget that failure is not a stumbling block; it's a stepping stone towards your greatness. Embrace it, learn from it, and let it propel you forward on your journey of growth and self-improvement. You've got this!

VISUALISING SUCCESS:

Visualizing success is a powerful tool, and it's something you can use to bring your dreams and goals to life. It's like creating a vivid mental movie of your future achievements, and it helps you stay focused and motivated on your path to success.

However, create a vivid mental image of your purpose fulfilled. Visualization is a powerful tool to keep your focus and motivation intact. Envision yourself living your purpose, achieving your goals, and making a positive impact. This mental rehearsal strengthens your belief in what's possible, making it easier to persevere through obstacles. Here's how you can make visualization work for you; First, find a quiet and comfortable space where you won't be disturbed. Close your eyes and take a few deep breaths to relax your mind and body. Now, picture yourself in the future, standing right at the moment when you've achieved your goal. It could be landing your dream job, acing an exam, or accomplishing a personal milestone - whatever it is, imagine it with all the details.

As you visualize, make it as detailed and realistic as possible. See the colours, hear the sounds, and feel the emotions of that moment. Imagine the smile on your face, the joy in your heart, and the sense of accomplishment that washes over you.

You are the star of this mental movie, and you're shining bright in your success. Feel the pride and satisfaction of knowing that all your hard work and dedication have paid off.

But don't stop there, my friend. Visualization goes beyond just the end result. Imagine the steps you took to get there. See yourself putting in the effort, facing challenges with determination, and overcoming obstacles with resilience. Visualize the small victories and progress you make along the way. Celebrate each milestone and use those moments of success as fuel to keep going. You see, by visualizing success, you create a roadmap in your mind. It's like having a GPS guiding you towards your goals. Your subconscious mind doesn't know the difference between reality and imagination, so when you vividly picture your success, it starts to believe in the possibility of achieving it.

This newfound belief gives you the confidence to take action and stay committed to your dreams. When you encounter setbacks or doubts, you can return to this visualization to remind yourself of your capabilities and the bright future that awaits you. Believe in yourself, trust the process, and let visualization be the compass that guides you towards the life you envision. With each mental picture, you'll be one step closer to turning your dreams into a beautiful reality. You have the ability to create the life you desire, and visualization is the key that unlocks your full potential. Embrace it, and let your dreams take flight!

REVISITING YOUR "WHY":

Revisiting your "why" is like reconnecting with the heart of your purpose, my friend. It's about taking the time to pause and reflect on the reasons that drive you on this meaningful journey. As time goes by, your sense of purpose might evolve. Periodically, take a moment to revisit your "why" - the reason driving your journey. Reconnecting with your purpose reinforces your determination and helps you adapt to any shifts in direction that might be necessary.
You see, as you navigate through life and pursue your dreams, it's natural for the path to evolve and change. In the midst of all the hustle and bustle, it's easy to lose sight of your original motivations. That's where revisiting your "why" becomes essential. Imagine yourself sitting in a quiet space, just you and your thoughts. Take a deep breath and ask yourself, "Why am I doing what I'm doing? What inspired me to start this journey in the first place?" Your answers to these questions form the core of your "why." By revisiting your "why," you rekindle the passion that fuels your purpose. It's like igniting a flame within your soul, reminding you of the deeper meaning behind your actions.
When you remember your "why," it brings clarity to your goals and helps you realign your priorities. You start to focus on what truly matters to you, and it becomes easier to let go of distractions and stay on track. Your "why" becomes the anchor that keeps you steady in the storm, guiding you through difficult moments and motivating you to keep moving forward.
By doing this, you ensure that your journey remains aligned with your heart's desires. You can make any necessary adjustments to your path, staying true to your authentic self. Your "why" holds the key to living a life of fulfillment and meaning. Embrace it, cherish it, and let it shine brightly as you embark on this beautiful journey of self-discovery and purposeful living. You've got this, and your "why" will always be there to light your way!

RECHARGING YOUR SPIRIT:

Recharging your spirit is like giving yourself a much-needed dose of positivity and vitality, my friend. It's about taking care of your inner self and nurturing the very essence of who you are. Amidst the persistence and effort, don't forget to take care of your well-being. Rest, relaxation, and self-care are essential to maintain the energy needed to persevere. Nurture your mind, body, and spirit to keep the fire of purpose burning brightly. Life can be demanding and fast-paced, and sometimes it's easy to neglect your emotional and spiritual well-being in the midst of it all. That's why it's crucial to make time for yourself, specifically for recharging your spirit.
Think of it as a soulful retreat, a moment of quiet reflection and self-care. You see, you have to be your own advocate for well-being. So, find a peaceful space where you can be alone with your thoughts, and let the healing process begin. During this time, engage in activities that bring you joy and inner peace. It could be taking a walk in nature, practicing meditation, or simply immersing yourself in your favorite hobby. Whatever it is, make sure it resonates

with your soul and replenishes your energy. Disconnect from the outside world for a while. Turn off your phone, step away from social media, and let yourself breathe. This break from external distractions allows you to focus on yourself and recharge without any unnecessary noise.

Recharging your spirit also involves self-reflection. Take some time to ponder on your emotions and thoughts. Acknowledge any stress or negativity you might be carrying and explore ways to release them. During this process, practice self-compassion. Be gentle with yourself and allow yourself to feel whatever emotions come up. Embrace them as part of being human, and remember that it's okay to take a step back and recharge when needed. You are your most significant source of strength, and taking care of your spirit is vital for your overall well-being. When you recharge your spirit, you open yourself up to a renewed sense of clarity and positivity. As you take care of your spirit, you cultivate a strong foundation for living a life of purpose, fulfillment, and joy. So go ahead, my friend, carve out that sacred space for yourself and let your spirit soar free. You have the power to nurture your soul and create a life that's truly meaningful. Recharge your spirit, and let it guide you on this beautiful journey of self-discovery and growth. So, don't forget to prioritize yourself and make time for recharging your spirit regularly. You deserve this time of rejuvenation and self-care. Embrace it, cherish it, and let it be a reminder of your own inner power.

WRITING YOUR STORY:

Writing your story is like painting a masterpiece with the brush of your experiences, my friend. It's about taking the pen in your hand and crafting the narrative of your life, a tale that is uniquely yours to tell. However, your journey of perseverance on the path of purpose is unique and worth documenting. Keep a journal to chronicle your experiences, challenges, and growth. In moments of doubt, you can revisit your journal and see how far you've come. You see, you are the author of your story, and each chapter unfolds with every decision, triumph, and challenge you encounter. No one else can write your story, for it is the beautiful tapestry of your hopes, dreams, and aspirations. So, take that blank page and let your imagination soar. Reflect on the moments that have shaped you, the people who have touched your heart, and the lessons that have left an indelible mark on your soul. Your story is not just about the grand accomplishments, but also about the small moments that make life meaningful. Cherish the simple joys, the laughter, and the connections that bring warmth to your heart. Moreover, don't forget that you have the power to create the future chapters of your story. Dream big, my friend, and let your aspirations guide you towards new adventures and possibilities. Write your story with courage and authenticity. Embrace your uniqueness, for it's the very essence that makes your story extraordinary. Trust yourself, and let your intuition be your guide as you navigate the twists and turns that life may bring.

With every word you write, you're creating a legacy that will live on, shaping the narrative of your life for generations to come. Embrace the power of your story, and let it be a beacon of hope and inspiration for the world to see. You have the pen in your hand; now, go and create a story that will leave a lasting impact on the world. Your story matters, and you have the power to make it a masterpiece.

In conclusion, embarking on the path of purpose is a transformative journey that grants you a profound sense of meaning and fulfillment. As you navigate through life's twists and turns, remember that perseverance is your steadfast ally, supporting you through the inevitable challenges and setbacks. It is your unwavering determination that will keep you moving forward, even when the road seems daunting.

Discovering and embracing your purpose requires courage, self-reflection, and a willingness to venture into the unknown. Embrace failures as stepping stones to growth, and practice self-compassion to stay resilient in the face of adversity. Cultivate mindfulness to remain grounded in the present moment and visualize success as you progress towards your goals. In your pursuit of purpose, remember that you are not alone. Build a support system of like-minded individuals who believe in your dreams and encourage you to persevere. Celebrate your milestones, however big or small, as each one represents progress on your journey. Let patience be your guiding light, for meaningful achievements take time to unfold. Be flexible and open to adapting your approach when necessary, for sometimes the path may take unexpected turns that lead to even greater opportunities. Your purposeful journey is a unique and beautiful story waiting to be written. Embrace the experiences, challenges, and growth along the way. Cherish the present moment and find joy in every step you take towards your purpose, for the journey itself holds tremendous value.

CHAPTER EIGHT

Embracing Imperfections and Finding Gratitude

"The journey of a thousand miles begins with a single step. Embrace every challenge, for within them lie the seeds of your success."

Life is a rollercoaster ride filled with ups and downs, twists, and turns. Sometimes, we find ourselves striving for perfection, whether it's in our relationships, careers, or personal growth. However, the pursuit of perfection can be exhausting and disheartening. What if I told you that embracing imperfections and finding gratitude is the key to a more fulfilling and contented life? Let's explore this transformative journey together. But before then let's look at the story of Ruth Martin was known for her warm smile, kind heart, and a remarkable talent for growing the most beautiful flowers in her garden.

Every morning, Ruth would wake up before the sun, don her favorite straw hat, and tend to her garden with unwavering dedication. The townspeople would often gather near her home just to catch a glimpse of the vibrant array of flowers that adorned her yard.

One day, a travelling florist named Lily arrived in the town. Lily had heard whispers of Ruth's remarkable garden and was eager to see it for herself. As she approached Ruth's home, she was awe-struck by the kaleidoscope of colours that greeted her. Lily knew she had stumbled upon a hidden treasure.

Curiosity got the best of her, and Lily decided to introduce herself to the woman responsible for the stunning display. She knocked on Ruth's door, and the moment it opened, she was met with the same warm smile she had heard so much about.

Ruth welcomed Lily inside and offered her a cup of herbal tea. As they sat in Ruth's cozy living room, Lily couldn't help but ask the secret to her thriving garden. Ruth chuckled softly and said, "Patience and love, my dear. Each flower is like a child to me, and I tend to them with care and devotion."

They spent hours talking about their shared passion for flowers and the joy it brought them. Lily realized that she had found more than just a remarkable garden; she had found a kindred spirit in Ruth.

In the end, Ruth's garden won the first prize, and she received the recognition she truly deserved. Her heart was filled with gratitude for Lily, whose belief in her talents had opened doors she had never dreamed of.

As the years passed, Ruth's garden continued to flourish, but her greatest treasure remained her friendship with Lily. Their shared love for flowers had brought them together, and their bond grew stronger with each passing season. The tale of Ruth Martin's garden and her cherished friendship with Lily became a legend in the town. To this day, people visit the little town to admire the blooming masterpiece that was once just a reflection of a humble woman's passion, love, and gratitude. And at the heart of it all was Ruth Martin, the gardener with a warm smile and a heart full of love for the beauty that surrounded her.

Now let's delve into the transformative journey of gratitude and imperfection. Let's talk about gratitude and the incredible power it holds in your life. You might have heard the phrase "count your blessings," and that's exactly what gratitude is all about – appreciating and acknowledging the positive aspects of your life, no matter how big or small they may seem.

You see, gratitude is like a superpower that can bring immense joy and contentment into your daily existence. When you practice gratitude, you shift your focus from what's lacking in your life to what you already have. It's like flipping a switch in your mind that allows you to see the beauty and abundance all around you.

So, how can you tap into the power of gratitude? It's quite simple, really. Take a moment each day to pause and reflect on the things you're thankful for. It could be the support of your friends and family, the opportunities that come your way, the little acts of kindness you receive, or even the beauty of nature surrounding you.

When you express gratitude, you create a positive ripple effect in your life. You start to attract more positive experiences and relationships because gratitude shifts your energy towards a more positive and appreciative state of mind. It also helps you cope with challenges and setbacks, making you more resilient and optimistic.

Think of gratitude as a magnifying glass that amplifies the goodness in your life. The more you count your blessings, the more blessings you'll notice coming your way. It's like a beautiful cycle of positivity and abundance. Practicing gratitude doesn't mean ignoring the tough times or pretending that everything is perfect. It's about finding the silver lining even in difficult situations. By acknowledging the lessons and growth that come from challenges, you can develop a deeper sense of gratitude for the strength and resilience you gain.

Incorporating gratitude into your daily routine can be as simple as keeping a gratitude journal. Each day, jot down a few things you're grateful for – it could be the laughter shared with a friend, a delicious meal, or the warm rays of the sun on your face. Taking the time to acknowledge and appreciate these moments will fill your heart with a sense of contentment and joy. Remember, gratitude is a practice, and like any skill, it becomes stronger and more profound with consistency. So, why not start today? Take a moment to think about the blessings in your life, and feel the positive energy that comes with gratitude. Embrace the power of counting your blessings, and you'll discover a whole new world of happiness and fulfillment right at your fingertips.

Absolutely! Let's talk about finding gratitude in adversity and why it can be a powerful mindset to adopt in challenging times. You know, life is full of ups and downs, and adversity is something we all face at various points in our journey. It can be tough, disheartening, and overwhelming, but amidst the struggles, finding gratitude can be a transformative way to navigate through difficult situations.

When you find gratitude in adversity, you're not denying the challenges you're facing or pretending that everything is perfect. Instead, you're choosing to look beyond the hardships and see the silver lining in the midst of the storm. It's about shifting your perspective and finding moments of appreciation, even in the darkest times. You might wonder, "How can I find gratitude when everything feels so tough?" Well, it starts with acknowledging your emotions and giving yourself permission to feel what you're feeling. It's okay to be sad, angry, or frustrated in difficult times. But once you've acknowledged those emotions, try to shift your focus to the things you can be grateful for.

For example, in times of adversity, you can be grateful for the support and love of your friends and family who are there for you, offering a shoulder to lean on. You can find gratitude in the lessons you're learning through the challenges, knowing that they will make you stronger and wiser. You can appreciate the small moments of joy or kindness that brighten your day, even amidst the struggles.

Finding gratitude in adversity can also be about finding a sense of purpose or meaning in difficult situations. It's about asking yourself, "What can I learn from this experience? How can I grow as a person? How can I use this challenge to make a positive impact?"

Moreover, it's perfectly normal to have moments when gratitude feels hard to come by. In those moments, remember that gratitude doesn't have to be a grand gesture; it can be as simple as finding gratitude for having a roof over your head, a warm meal, or the ability to take a deep breath.

Practicing gratitude in adversity can be a powerful tool to shift your mindset from a victim mentality to one of resilience and empowerment. When you find gratitude, you reclaim your inner strength and find the courage to face challenges head-on. It's like finding a light in the darkness, guiding you towards hope and a sense of peace amidst turmoil.

You don't have to wait for everything to be perfect to find gratitude. It's about finding those glimmers of positivity, no matter how small, and letting them brighten your path. So, my friend, in times of adversity, be gentle with yourself, acknowledge the hardships, and then open your heart to the possibility of finding gratitude. It might not be easy, but with practice and self-compassion, you'll discover the power of gratitude to transform your perspective and lead you towards a more resilient and hopeful outlook on life. Of course! You know, when it comes to your career and the dreams you have, it's easy to put a lot of pressure on yourself to be perfect. But the truth is, no one is flawless, and that's okay – including you.

Embracing imperfections in your career means accepting that you won't have all the answers right away, and that's completely normal. It's about understanding that making mistakes or facing setbacks doesn't make you a failure. Instead, those experiences are opportunities for growth and learning.

In your career, you'll encounter challenges, moments of uncertainty, and maybe even some detours along the way. But remember, those imperfections are stepping stones to success. They allow you to learn valuable lessons, gain new skills, and discover what truly matters to you.

It's easy to compare yourself to others in your field, thinking they have it all figured out while you're still finding your way. But, my friend, comparing your journey to someone else's is not fair to you. Each person's path is unique, and everyone faces their share of imperfections. Instead of aiming for unattainable perfection, focus on progress. Set realistic goals for yourself and celebrate each step forward, no matter how small. Recognize that growth and development take time, and it's okay to take detours or change your mind along the way. Your career is not a straight line, and that's what makes it exciting and full of possibilities.

Moreover, embrace the imperfections in your ambitions. Your dreams might evolve or shift as you gain new experiences and insights. Allow yourself to explore different paths and be open to unexpected opportunities. Your ambitions might not follow a linear path, and that's alright – it's all part of the beautiful chaos of life.

Lastly, be kind to yourself when you encounter setbacks or face challenges. Instead of criticizing yourself for not being perfect, view those moments as opportunities for growth and improvement. Celebrate your resilience and determination to keep moving forward, even when things get tough.

My advice to you on embracing imperfections and finding gratitude:

1. **Be Kind to Yourself:** Remember that nobody is perfect, and that's okay. Treat yourself with the same kindness and understanding you would offer a friend who

makes a mistake. Embrace your imperfections as a natural part of being human and use them as opportunities for growth and learning.

2. **Shift Your Perspective:** Instead of viewing imperfections as failures, see them as stepping stones on your journey to success. Each challenge and setback is an opportunity to develop resilience and gain valuable experience. Embrace the process and trust that it's all leading you to where you're meant to be.

3. **Avoid Comparison:** Comparing yourself to others can rob you of gratitude and lead to feelings of inadequacy. Focus on your own journey and the unique blessings in your life. Remember that gratitude thrives when you appreciate what you have, not when you long for what others possess.

4. **Practice Daily Gratitude:** Take a few minutes each day to reflect on the things you're grateful for. Write them down in a journal or simply say them out loud. This practice will help you shift your focus from what's lacking to what's abundant in your life.

Because, incorporating the practice of embracing imperfections and finding gratitude into your daily life can bring a profound shift in your mindset and overall well-being. Embrace the beauty of imperfection and the richness of gratitude, and you'll discover a newfound sense of peace, self-acceptance, and joy. Remember, it's a journey, so be patient with yourself, and enjoy the process of growth and self-discovery.

Let's talk about gratitude for simple pleasures, because it's a beautiful way to find joy and contentment in your everyday life. You know, sometimes we get so caught up in our busy routines and big aspirations that we overlook the small, wonderful moments that surround us.

Gratitude for simple pleasures is all about taking a moment to pause and appreciate the little things that bring happiness to your heart. It's like finding delight in the ordinary, everyday moments that often go unnoticed. By doing so, you can add a dose of positivity and mindfulness to your daily routine.

So, what are some of these simple pleasures that you can be grateful for? Well, it could be the aroma of freshly brewed coffee in the morning, the warmth of the sun on your face during a walk, or the sound of laughter shared with loved ones. It might be the joy of curling up with a good book, the taste of your favorite meal, or the feeling of soft grass beneath your feet.

Finding gratitude for these simple pleasures is like unwrapping a gift each day. It's about savouring the present moment and recognizing the beauty that surrounds you, even in the smallest of things.

Remember, these moments might seem insignificant at first, but when you acknowledge and appreciate them, they add richness and meaning to your life. Gratitude for simple pleasures also helps to shift your focus from what's lacking to what's abundant in your life. It's a wonderful way to cultivate a positive outlook and a sense of contentment.

Without a doubt! Let's talk about mindfulness and meditation, two important practices that can help you live a more peaceful and clear life. Mindfulness and meditation act as anchors, keeping you present and centred in the midst of daily chaos.

Mindfulness is all about being fully engaged and aware of the present moment. It's about paying attention to your thoughts, emotions, and sensations without judgement. When you practice mindfulness, you become an observer of your experiences, allowing you to respond to life's challenges with greater clarity and calmness.

You see, being mindful means that you're not dwelling on the past or anxiously anticipating the future. Instead, you're fully immersed in the here and now, appreciating each moment as it unfolds. It's like savouring the taste of your favorite meal, feeling the warmth of a hug from a loved one, or enjoying the simple pleasure of a deep breath.

Mindfulness is not about eradicating negative thoughts or emotions; it's about accepting them as part of the human experience. By doing so, you can gain a deeper understanding of yourself and your reactions, allowing you to respond to life's challenges in a more balanced and compassionate way.

Meditation, on the other hand, is a formal practice that enhances mindfulness. It's like training your mind to be more focused and aware. During meditation, you typically sit comfortably, close your eyes, and direct your attention to a specific point of focus, such as your breath or a particular mantra.

As you meditate, you'll inevitably encounter wandering thoughts, and that's completely normal. The key is to gently guide your attention back to your chosen focal point, building your capacity to stay present and focused.

Meditation allows you to cultivate a sense of inner stillness and tranquility. It can help reduce stress, improve concentration, and promote emotional well-being. With regular meditation practice, you'll notice that you become more in tune with your thoughts and emotions, and you'll develop a greater sense of self-awareness. Both mindfulness and meditation are skills that can be developed and deepened over time. As you engage in these practices, you'll find that you become more attuned to the beauty of each moment, and you'll experience a greater sense of peace and harmony within yourself.

Absolutely! Let's talk about positive affirmations, which are a powerful tool for changing your mentality and increasing your self-esteem. Positive affirmations are self-talk that can have a significant impact on your ideas and emotions. Positive affirmations are simple statements that reflect the qualities or outcomes you want to manifest in your life. They are written in the present tense, as if they are already true, and they are framed in a positive and affirmative way. For example, you can say, "I am confident and capable," "I attract abundance into my life," or "I embrace challenges as opportunities for growth."

The power of positive affirmations lies in their ability to rewire your thought patterns. You might have experienced moments of self-doubt or negative self-talk, but by repeating positive affirmations, you can replace those limiting beliefs with empowering ones.

When you say positive affirmations with conviction, you send a powerful message to your subconscious mind. Your subconscious then starts to align your thoughts, emotions, and actions with the affirmations you repeat. It's like programming your mind for success, self-love, and a positive outlook on life.

You can practice positive affirmations anytime, anywhere. You can say them out loud, write them in a journal, or repeat them silently in your mind. The key is to be consistent and make them a part of your daily routine.

Incorporating positive affirmations into your life can be particularly helpful during challenging times. They serve as a source of encouragement and support, reminding you of your inner strength and resilience.

Remember, positive affirmations are not about denying challenges or pretending everything is perfect. Instead, they are about empowering yourself to face challenges with a positive and determined mindset.

Absolutely! Let's discuss finding thankfulness in material simplicity, because it's a lovely way to appreciate the riches in your life. In today's culture, you know, there can be a lot of emphasis on material belongings and the desire for more. Finding thankfulness in material simplicity, on the other hand, is about appreciating what you currently have and finding contentment in the smallest of things. When you find gratitude in material simplicity, you're not chasing after the latest gadgets, the trendiest clothes, or the fanciest possessions. Instead, you're appreciating the basics and the essentials that bring comfort and joy to your life.

Take a moment to look around you and notice the simple pleasures you might overlook – the cozy blanket that keeps you warm, the delicious meal on your plate, the roof over your head that provides shelter. These are all material things that we often take for granted, but they are the foundation of a comfortable and meaningful life.

Gratitude in material simplicity is about recognizing that happiness does not solely come from the accumulation of things, but from the value you place on what you already possess. It's appreciating the quality of your belongings rather than the quantity. You can start practicing gratitude in material simplicity by decluttering your space and letting go of things you no longer need. This creates room for the things that truly bring you joy and serve a purpose in your life.

Moreover, finding gratitude in material simplicity is about focusing on experiences rather than possessions. Invest in creating memories and building connections with loved ones. These experiences can be far more fulfilling and long-lasting than any material possession.

By embracing material simplicity, you free yourself from the pressure of constantly seeking more and open your heart to the abundance that already surrounds you. You become less attached to possessions and more connected to the moments that truly matter. Remember, gratitude in material simplicity is not about depriving yourself of things you desire, but about finding contentment in what you already have. It's about shifting your perspective from "I need more" to "I have enough." Embrace the joy and contentment that comes from valuing what you already possess. You'll discover that true abundance is not in the quantity of your possessions, but in the gratitude and appreciation you cultivate for the simple things that enrich your life. Finding gratitude in material simplicity can lead you to a more fulfilling and meaningful existence, filled with contentment and appreciation for the little blessings that make life extraordinary.

In conclusion, embracing imperfections and finding gratitude is a life-long practice that allows you to live with greater authenticity, compassion, and contentment. It's about accepting yourself and others as beautifully imperfect beings, acknowledging that the journey towards growth and self-discovery is full of twists and turns. By embracing imperfections, you free yourself from the chains of perfectionism and self-criticism, allowing room for self-love, self-compassion, and personal growth. As you continue on this journey, remember that each day presents new opportunities to find gratitude in the simplest of moments and to celebrate progress, no matter how small. Embrace your unique self, let go of unrealistic expectations, and appreciate the beauty in the imperfect and messy aspects of life. As you do so, you'll find that embracing imperfections and finding gratitude can lead you to a more fulfilling and meaningful existence, enriching your relationships, and deepening your connection with yourself and the world around you.

CHAPTER NINE

<u>Heal with Forgiveness & Compassion</u>

"Small actions lead to big results - take one step at a time, and you'll reach the mountaintop."

You've been carrying the weight of resentment, hurt, and disappointment for far too long. The burden of these negative emotions has left you feeling drained, isolated, and unable to move forward. But there is a path to healing, and it begins with two powerful tools: forgiveness and compassion. As you embark on this transformative journey, you'll discover how these profound qualities can set you free from the chains of bitterness and lead you towards lasting inner peace.

First and foremost, you must understand that forgiveness is not about condoning the actions of others or dismissing the pain they caused you. Instead, it's a gift you give to yourself, a decision to release the hold that the past has on your present and future. By forgiving, you release the power those who wronged you once held over your emotions and reclaim your autonomy. Think about a painful event from your past - an old wound that still stings when you think about it. Now, close your eyes, take a deep breath, and imagine forgiveness flowing through you like a warm, soothing light. With every exhale, visualize yourself letting go of the pain, resentment, and anger you've been harbouring. As you open your eyes, you'll notice a subtle shift in your perspective - a newfound sense of freedom and empowerment.

Compassion is the second vital element in your healing journey. It involves not only extending understanding and empathy to others but, crucially, offering it to yourself. Often, we are our harshest critics, dwelling on our mistakes and shortcomings. But practicing self-compassion means treating yourself with the same kindness you would show a dear friend facing a difficult situation. Next time you find yourself berating yourself for a perceived failure or setback, pause for a moment. Imagine you're speaking to a friend experiencing the same challenges. What would you say to them? Extend those same words of support and encouragement to yourself. Embrace your imperfections, acknowledge that everyone makes mistakes, and remember that your worth is not defined by any missteps you might have taken.

Incorporating self-compassion into your life may take time, but it will undoubtedly pave the way for a healthier relationship with yourself. As you grow more compassionate, you'll find it easier to extend that compassion to others, no matter their past actions or beliefs.

Recognize that everyone is on their journey, carrying their burdens, and seeking their own paths to healing. One way to strengthen your compassion is by practicing loving-kindness meditation. Find a comfortable, quiet space, close your eyes, and repeat phrases like, "May I be happy, may I be healthy, may I be safe, may I live with ease." Then, extend these wishes to others: "May you be happy, may you be healthy, may you be safe, may you live with ease." By doing this, you open your heart to love and empathy, fostering a more profound connection with the world around you.

One of the most profound effects of forgiveness and compassion is their ability to break the cycle of negativity. By releasing the grip of anger and resentment, you create space for positive emotions to emerge. As you let go of old wounds, you'll notice that your heart becomes lighter, and a newfound sense of peace settles within you.

Moreover, healing through forgiveness and compassion can lead to better relationships with those around you. When you practice forgiveness, it doesn't necessarily mean forgetting the past but rather not allowing it to dictate your present interactions. This openness allows for more genuine connections with others, fostering an environment of trust and understanding. Of course, it's important to note that forgiveness does not necessarily mean reconciliation. You may choose to forgive someone, but it doesn't mean you must continue a relationship with them if it's unhealthy or toxic. Forgiveness is about freeing yourself from the emotional burden, and you can do so while still maintaining healthy boundaries. Continuing on this journey of healing with forgiveness and compassion, you'll start to notice subtle yet profound changes in various aspects of your life. Let's explore some of the specific ways these powerful qualities can positively impact your well-being:

1. EMOTIONAL LIBERATION:

Emotional liberation, in its essence, is about freeing yourself from the chains of negative emotions that weigh you down and hold you back. It's a journey of self-discovery and healing where you allow yourself to release the burdens of past hurts and resentments, granting yourself the gift of emotional freedom.

Forgiving others and yourself allows you to release the heavy emotional baggage you've been carrying. As you let go of resentment and anger, you create space for more positive emotions like joy, love, and gratitude. You'll find yourself more at peace and less overwhelmed by negative emotions.

Imagine carrying a heavy backpack filled with all the painful memories, grudges, and unresolved emotions from your past. Each step you take feels harder as the weight of these negative emotions presses on your shoulders. This burden impacts your interactions with others, colours your perception of the world, and prevents you from fully embracing the present moment.

Now, picture yourself unzipping that backpack and slowly taking out each emotional weight you've been carrying. With each emotion you release, you feel a little lighter, a little freer. As you let go of old hurts and forgive those who have wronged you, you begin to experience emotional liberation.

Emotional liberation means breaking free from the grip of past wounds, no longer allowing them to dictate how you feel or behave in the present. It doesn't mean erasing the memories or pretending that the pain didn't exist. Instead, it's a conscious choice to acknowledge those emotions, process them, and then release them, creating space for healing and growth.

When you achieve emotional liberation, you'll notice a shift in how you respond to challenging situations. Instead of reacting from a place of hurt and anger, you'll approach conflicts with a sense of calmness and understanding. It empowers you to choose love and empathy, even in difficult circumstances, and to focus on solutions rather than dwelling on problems.

This process of emotional liberation also involves extending compassion and forgiveness to yourself. Often, we hold onto self-criticism and guilt for past mistakes or perceived shortcomings. Emotional liberation invites you to embrace self-compassion, recognizing that you're human, and it's okay to make mistakes. By forgiving yourself and being kind to yourself, you free your heart from self-inflicted pain.

Emotional liberation is not an overnight process; it takes time and effort. But with each step you take, with each emotion you release, you'll come closer to feeling emotionally free. It's a journey worth embarking on - a journey that empowers you to reclaim your emotional well-being, embrace the present with open arms, and create a brighter and more fulfilling future.

2. IMPROVED MENTAL HEALTH:

Improved mental health is a journey of self-care and understanding that allows you to nurture your mind, emotions, and overall well-being. It's about prioritizing your mental health and taking steps to cultivate a positive and resilient mindset. When you focus on improving your mental health, you empower yourself to lead a more fulfilling and balanced life.

As you cultivate forgiveness and compassion, you'll likely experience improved mental health. Letting go of past hurts can alleviate symptoms of anxiety, depression, and even post-traumatic stress disorder (PTSD). Compassion, both towards yourself and others, can act as a buffer against self-criticism and negative thought patterns. You see, your mental health is just as important as your physical health - it's a crucial aspect of your overall wellness. When you take care of your mental health, you're nurturing the core of who you are, the thoughts and feelings that shape your experiences.

So, how can you improve your mental health? First and foremost, it's essential to recognize and acknowledge your emotions. Instead of brushing them aside or pretending they don't exist, give yourself permission to feel what you feel. Emotions are a natural part of being human, and allowing yourself to experience them without judgement is a powerful act of self-compassion.

Next, take time to practice self-care regularly. This means making space for activities that bring you joy and relaxation. Whether it's spending time in nature, engaging in a hobby, reading a book, or meditating, these moments of self-nurturing can help reduce stress and increase your overall sense of well-being.

Furthermore, be mindful of your thoughts and the stories you tell yourself. Negative thought patterns can impact your mental health, leading to increased anxiety and self-doubt. When you catch yourself engaging in negative self-talk, pause, and challenge those thoughts. Replace them with more positive and affirming statements.

Another crucial aspect of improving your mental health is seeking support when needed. Remember that it's okay to ask for help - you don't have to navigate life's challenges alone. Reach out to friends, family, or a professional counsellor if you find yourself struggling with overwhelming emotions or situations. Talking to someone can provide valuable insights, guidance, and a sense of relief.

Incorporating regular physical activity into your routine can also significantly impact your mental health. Exercise has been shown to release feel-good chemicals in the brain, such as endorphins, which can help reduce stress and improve your mood. Whether it's going for a walk, dancing, or practicing yoga, find an activity that you enjoy and can do regularly.

Moreover, pay attention to your sleep habits. Quality sleep is essential for mental health and overall well-being. Establish a consistent sleep schedule, create a relaxing bedtime routine, and ensure your sleeping environment is comfortable and conducive to rest.

Lastly, remember that healing and improving mental health is a journey, not a destination. Be patient with yourself as you navigate this path of growth and self-discovery. Celebrate the progress you make, no matter how small, and be gentle with yourself during setbacks.

By prioritizing your mental health and taking active steps to nurture it, you'll find yourself better equipped to handle life's challenges and embrace its joys. Improved mental health allows you to cultivate a positive and resilient mindset, fostering a greater sense of balance and fulfillment in your daily life. You deserve to invest in your mental well-being, and by doing so, you empower yourself to lead a more joyful, meaningful, and vibrant life.

3. EMPOWERMENT:

Empowerment is all about recognizing your innate strength and potential, and using that awareness to take control of your life and choices. It's about stepping into your own power, embracing your unique qualities, and believing in yourself wholeheartedly. When you empower yourself, you become the author of your own story, capable of creating the life you desire.

Forgiveness is a choice that empowers you to take control of your emotions and reactions. Instead of being a victim of past circumstances, you become the architect of your own healing and growth.

You see, empowerment starts with a mindset shift - a shift that says, "I have the ability to shape my own destiny." It's about letting go of limiting beliefs and self-doubt, and instead, choosing to focus on your strengths and capabilities. When you believe in yourself, you become unstoppable, breaking free from the chains of fear and insecurity.

Empowerment means taking responsibility for your decisions and actions. It's understanding that you have the power to make choices that align with your values and aspirations. You are not bound by the expectations of others or the constraints of your past. Instead, you have the freedom to pave your own path and define success on your terms.

Take a moment to reflect on your dreams and aspirations. What are the goals you've been longing to achieve? Now, imagine yourself embracing your power and setting these goals into motion. Visualize yourself taking confident steps towards your dreams, overcoming obstacles with determination, and celebrating your achievements along the way. This is the essence of empowerment - the ability to turn your vision into reality.

Empowerment is not just about personal growth; it's also about uplifting and supporting others. When you feel empowered, you become a beacon of inspiration for those around you. Your self-assurance and determination serve as a catalyst for positive change, encouraging others to embrace their own power and potential.

Moreover, empowerment involves setting healthy boundaries in your relationships. You have the right to prioritize your needs, desires, and well-being. By communicating assertively and respectfully, you establish boundaries that honour your values and protect your emotional space.

Remember that empowerment is not about seeking external validation or comparing yourself to others. It's about embracing your unique journey and understanding that your worth is not determined by external factors. When you cultivate self-empowerment, you'll find that your self-esteem and confidence blossom from within.

Of course, the journey of empowerment may encounter obstacles, and that's perfectly normal. Life is full of challenges, but with empowerment on your side, you'll face them with resilience and courage. You'll discover that setbacks are opportunities for growth and learning, and each experience contributes to your personal development. So, embrace your power, believe in yourself, and know that you have everything it takes to create a life filled with purpose and fulfillment. You are capable of achieving your dreams, impacting others positively, and navigating the twists and turns of life with grace and strength.

Empowerment is not an endpoint; it's an ongoing process of self-discovery and growth. Embrace it as a lifelong journey, and with every step you take, you'll find yourself becoming more confident, more resilient, and more connected to your authentic self. The power to empower yourself lies within you - it's time to unlock that potential and embark on a transformative path of self-empowerment. You are worthy, capable, and deserving of living a life empowered by your dreams and aspirations. Embrace your power, and let it guide you towards a future filled with endless possibilities.

4. LETTING GO OF THE PAST:

Letting go of the past is a powerful act of self-liberation that empowers you to move forward with a lighter heart and a renewed sense of freedom. It's about releasing the emotional baggage that has been weighing you down and holding you back from fully embracing the present and creating a brighter future.

Dwelling on past grievances can keep you stuck in a cycle of negativity. Embracing forgiveness allows you to break free from this cycle, focus on the present moment, and create a brighter future for yourself.

You know that feeling when you're holding onto something tightly, and it feels like a heavy burden on your shoulders? The past can be just like that - a collection of memories, regrets, and unresolved emotions that create a constant weight on your mind and soul.

But here's the thing, you have the power to let go. It starts with acknowledging that the past is unchangeable - what's done is done. You can't go back and rewrite history, but you can change how you relate to it in the present.

Ask yourself, what aspects of the past are you still holding onto? Are there past hurts, regrets, or grudges that you're carrying with you? Identify these emotional burdens, for it's the first step in the process of letting go. Now, take a deep breath, and visualize yourself setting down those heavy emotional weights, one by one. Imagine the relief and lightness you feel as you release these burdens. Remind yourself that holding onto the past doesn't serve you; it only keeps you stuck in a loop of negative emotions.

Letting go of the past doesn't mean forgetting or denying what happened. It's about finding acceptance and understanding that the past is a part of your journey, but it doesn't define who you are today.

One effective way to let go of the past is through forgiveness - both towards others and yourself. Forgiveness is not condoning what happened or letting someone off the hook; it's a gift you give yourself. When you forgive, you free yourself from the chains of resentment and anger, opening up space for healing and growth. You might also find it helpful to practice mindfulness - being fully present in the here and now. Mindfulness allows you to let go of ruminating thoughts about the past and worries about the future. By focusing on the present moment, you experience a sense of peace and clarity.

It's essential to be patient and gentle with yourself during this process of letting go. Healing takes time, and it's okay to take small steps. Celebrate every little breakthrough you make, and don't be too hard on yourself if you have setbacks. Remember, you are human, and it's natural to have ups and downs on this journey.

As you let go of the past, you create space for new experiences and opportunities. You become more open to embracing the present fully and creating a future that aligns with your true desires and aspirations.

Letting go of the past is an act of self-empowerment. It's a declaration that you are choosing to live in the present, unburdened by the weight of yesterday. Embrace this liberating process, and you'll find yourself stepping into a new chapter of your life - one filled with hope, joy, and the freedom to be authentically you. The power to let go lies within you, and it's time to embrace it and live life to the fullest.

In conclusion, the transformative journey of healing with forgiveness and compassion holds the key to unlocking a world of inner peace, emotional liberation, and genuine connections. As you embark on this path, you'll discover the profound impact of forgiveness - not as a means of condoning past actions, but as a gift of liberation you give to yourself. Through forgiveness, you release the grip of anger and resentment, paving the way for a heart that is lighter, more open, and free from the burdens of the past.

Compassion, both towards others and yourself, acts as a guiding light, illuminating the way to understanding and empathy. Embracing self-compassion allows you to be kinder to yourself, recognizing that you are worthy of love and forgiveness, despite any perceived imperfections. And as you extend compassion to others, you contribute to a world built on understanding, acceptance, and connection.

Throughout this journey, you'll encounter moments of growth and self-discovery, and it's important to remember that healing is a process, not an overnight transformation. Be patient with yourself, and allow yourself the time and space needed to heal fully. Celebrate each step forward, no matter how small, and be gentle with yourself during setbacks.

Healing with forgiveness and compassion empowers you to break free from the shackles of the past, to transcend negative emotions, and to embrace the present moment with an open heart. The emotional liberation you experience will lead to improved mental health, reduced stress, and increased resilience in the face of life's challenges.

As you nurture your emotional well-being, you'll find your relationships deepening, as communication becomes grounded in empathy and understanding. You'll become a source of inspiration, uplifting others through your acts of forgiveness, compassion, and kindness. Remember that this journey is unique to you, and there is no right or wrong way to embark on it. Embrace the power of forgiveness and compassion as your allies, guiding you towards lasting inner peace and a life filled with love and joy.

So, take that first step towards healing today. Open your heart to the transformative power of forgiveness and compassion. Embrace your own strength and resilience as you let go of the past, and create a future illuminated by the light of compassion and understanding. You are deserving of this journey, and as you heal yourself, you'll become a beacon of hope, radiating healing and positivity to those around you.

In the end, healing with forgiveness and compassion is an act of self-love, a courageous declaration that you are worthy of inner peace and emotional freedom. Embrace this transformative journey, and watch as the world around you begins to mirror the love and healing you cultivate within yourself. You have the power to heal, to forgive, and to love - now go forth and embrace the boundless possibilities that await on this beautiful path of healing with forgiveness and compassion.

To get more understanding on this topic, I recommend to you "How to inner peace" By Jerry Robert, I explained everything you'd like to know about forgiveness and self-compassion in it. The book is available on amazon platform.

CHAPTER TEN

Gratitude Mindset Journey

"Every day is a new chance to rewrite your future and create the life you desire."

Welcome to the journey of cultivating a gratitude mindset, where the power of thankfulness can transform your life in extraordinary ways. In this chapter, you will discover the countless benefits of practicing gratitude and how it can profoundly impact your thoughts, emotions, and overall well-being. By adopting a gratitude mindset, you will learn to appreciate the beauty of everyday moments, foster stronger relationships, and find greater resilience in the face of life's challenges. Let me take you on a quest, where you will unravel the secrets of recognizing the blessings that surround you. Picture yourself pausing each day to reflect on three precious things you are thankful for. It could be as trivial as the soft whispers of a gentle breeze or as meaningful as the unwavering support of a cherished friend. In these small yet mighty acts of gratitude, you will find solace, nourishing your soul with optimism and unveiling the abundance that often goes unnoticed.

Amidst the chaos of modern life, it's easy to lose touch with the present moment. However, a gratitude mindset offers the remedy—a precious key to unlocking mindful presence. Envision yourself cherishing each second of your daily experiences, savouring the taste of your morning coffee, fully immersed in the majesty of nature during a serene walk, and genuinely engaging in heartfelt conversations. As you embrace this mindful awareness, you will find yourself enchanted by the magic of gratitude that breathes life into otherwise ordinary moments.

But gratitude is not meant to be confined within the boundaries of our hearts; it craves expression. Imagine the joy of conveying your appreciation to others for their kindness, support, and contributions. Picture the smiles you bring to their faces as you offer a simple yet heartfelt "thank you." These sincere exchanges of gratitude kindle the flames of positivity and harmony, weaving a tapestry of meaningful connections that enrich your life immeasurably.

Now, let's explore the magic of a gratitude journal—a wondrous vessel that captures your grateful musings. Imagine the pleasure of pouring your thoughts onto paper, basking in the glow of positivity as you recount the blessings that have graced your life. With each stroke of the pen, you will find yourself entwined with gratitude's embrace, slowly unveiling a profound shift in your perspective—witnessing the world through the lens of appreciation.

In the crucible of adversity, you may be tempted to surrender to the weight of despair, but remember that gratitude can be your guiding light. Imagine finding solace in the darkest hours by seeking the hidden gems within trials. Let thankfulness kindle a spark of hope, empowering you to rise above challenges with newfound determination and courage.

Yet, as you traverse the path of gratitude, be wary of the traps of comparison that litter the road. Instead of measuring your life against others', picture yourself embracing your unique journey—celebrating each twist and turn, and finding contentment in your personal growth. For you are the master of your destiny, and in gratitude, you shall find the strength to flourish.

Gratitude blooms like a radiant flower, nourished by acts of kindness and compassion. Envision yourself lending a helping hand, volunteering your time, or supporting a friend in need. In these selfless gestures, you ignite a virtuous cycle of gratitude, wherein giving and receiving intertwine in a harmonious dance of interconnectedness.

Let's dive into the remarkable steps of the gratitude mindset.

STEP ONE. BE PATIENT AND PERSISTENT:

Let's talk about being patient and persistent, and how it applies to cultivating a gratitude mindset. You see, developing a gratitude mindset is not something that happens overnight. It's a journey, and just like any journey, it requires patience and persistence. So, let me break it down for you. Firstly, be patient with yourself. Remember that adopting a new mindset takes time and effort. You might not see immediate results, and that's perfectly okay. It's normal to have days when you feel more grateful than others, and that's all part of the process. So, don't be too hard on yourself if you find it challenging to be consistently grateful right from the start.

When you encounter obstacles or setbacks, don't get discouraged. Instead, be patient with the learning curve. You may encounter moments when you forget to practice gratitude or when negative thoughts try to take over. But that's where persistence comes in.

Persistence means sticking with it even when it's tough. It's about making a conscious effort to return to your gratitude practice even after you've faltered. So, if you miss a day of journaling or find it hard to find things to be grateful for, don't give up. Remind yourself of the benefits of a gratitude mindset, and recommit to practicing gratitude the next day.

Remember that gratitude is a skill, and like any skill, it improves with practice. The more you persist in your gratitude journey, the more natural it will become. You'll start noticing the positive changes it brings to your life—how it shifts your perspective, boosts your mood, and strengthens your relationships.

Being patient and persistent in cultivating a gratitude mindset also means celebrating the small victories. Acknowledge the moments when you genuinely feel grateful, no matter how fleeting they may seem. Each time you express gratitude, whether to yourself or to others, celebrate that as progress. It's these small steps that accumulate and build a foundation for a lasting gratitude mindset.

STEP TWO. USE VISUAL REMINDERS:

Visual reminders can be a powerful tool in cultivating your gratitude mindset, and they can make a significant difference in how you approach each day. Let me explain how you can use visual reminders to enhance your practice of gratitude. You know those moments when you get caught up in the busyness of life, and it's easy to forget about gratitude? Well, that's where visual reminders come in handy. Place little reminders in your living space or workspace—things like inspirational quotes, uplifting images, or even a small symbol that represents gratitude to you. By doing this, you create an environment that nurtures a grateful outlook.

Imagine waking up in the morning and seeing a beautiful framed quote about gratitude on your bedside table. As you start your day, that visual reminder serves as a gentle nudge to set a positive tone for the hours ahead. It can be as simple as a post-it note on your bathroom mirror with a reminder to think of one thing you're grateful for while getting ready for the day.

Now, let's think about your workspace. You could have a small gratitude journal or a gratitude jar on your desk. Whenever you have a moment, take a glance at it and jot down a few things you are thankful for. Those visual cues remind you to pause and appreciate the blessings that exist amidst your busy workday.

You can even use technology to your advantage. Set a screensaver on your phone or computer with a beautiful image related to gratitude. This way, every time you check your devices, you'll be greeted with a visual reminder of the importance of cultivating gratitude. Moreover, you can use nature to inspire your gratitude practice. How about placing a potted plant or a vase of fresh flowers in your living room? As you water the plant or admire the blooms, let it serve as a reminder to nurture your gratitude daily, just like you care for the plant's growth.

By integrating these visual reminders into your daily life, you create a supportive atmosphere for your gratitude mindset. These reminders act as gentle prompts, guiding you to pause, reflect, and embrace thankfulness throughout your day.

So, go ahead and personalize your visual reminders. Choose images, quotes, or symbols that resonate with you and evoke feelings of gratitude. Remember, the goal is to make them visible in places where you spend the most time. With these visual cues surrounding you, you'll find it easier to stay mindful of gratitude, even during the busiest and most challenging moments.

Incorporate visual reminders into your life, and witness the subtle yet profound impact they have on your gratitude practice. They will help you cultivate a deeper sense of appreciation for the beauty and abundance in your life, allowing you to infuse each day with a heart full of thankfulness.

STEP THREE. CULTIVATING MINDFUL PRESENCE:

Cultivating mindful presence is about immersing yourself fully in the present moment, and it's a transformative practice that can bring more clarity and contentment to your life. Let me explain how you can embrace mindful presence and make it a part of your daily experiences. First, picture yourself taking a few moments each day to intentionally focus on the here and now. You see, being present doesn't mean you have to block out all thoughts or distractions; it's about gently redirecting your attention to the present moment whenever your mind wanders. So, when you catch yourself drifting into thoughts about the past or worries about the future, bring your awareness back to the present with kindness and without judgement.

Now, let's talk about the power of your breath. You can use your breath as an anchor to keep you grounded in the present. Take a deep breath in, feel your lungs fill with air, and then slowly exhale. Pay attention to the sensations of your breath—its rhythm, temperature, and the gentle rise and fall of your chest. Doing this simple practice for even just a few minutes a day can help you cultivate mindful presence.

Imagine going for a walk and fully immersing yourself in the experience. Feel the earth beneath your feet, listen to the sounds around you—the chirping of birds, the rustling of leaves, the distant hum of traffic. As you walk, let go of any rushing thoughts and savour each step. Notice the subtle details of your surroundings—the colours, the textures, and the beauty that often goes unnoticed when you're preoccupied with worries or distractions.

You can also apply mindful presence to your daily activities. Whether it's washing the dishes, eating a meal, or even taking a shower, give your full attention to the task at hand. Feel the warmth of the water, the texture of the dishes, or the flavours of the food. When your mind starts to wander, gently bring it back to the sensations of the moment.

In social interactions, practice mindful presence by being fully engaged with the person you're talking to. Give them your undivided attention, listen actively, and be present with empathy and understanding. Put aside any distractions, like your phone or other thoughts, and truly connect with the other person in the here and now.

Remember, cultivating mindful presence is a skill that takes practice. Be patient with yourself, as your mind may wander frequently in the beginning. Each time you bring your attention back to the present, you strengthen your ability to be mindful.

By embracing mindful presence, you'll find that life becomes richer and more meaningful. You'll savour the little joys, notice the beauty in ordinary moments, and feel more grounded amidst the chaos of everyday life. So, give yourself the gift of mindful presence, and watch as it infuses your life with a sense of peace, gratitude, and profound awareness of the precious moments that unfold before you.

Now, let's look into the principles of a gratitude mindset revolve around adopting a positive and appreciative perspective towards life. This mindset is rooted in acknowledging and expressing thankfulness for the blessings, big or small, that surround us each day. Here are the key principles of cultivating a gratitude mindset:

- **Appreciation for Abundance:** Shift your focus from what you lack to what you already have. Cultivate a sense of appreciation for the abundance that exists in your life, whether it's good health, loving relationships, or simple pleasures.

- **Express Gratitude to Others:** Don't keep your gratitude to yourself. Express thanks and appreciation to the people who make a positive impact in your life. Show genuine appreciation for their kindness, support, and efforts.

- **Gratitude as a Way of Life:** Make gratitude a part of your daily interactions and activities. Let it shape your decisions, responses, and interactions with others, creating a positive ripple effect in your life and the lives of those around you.

- **Generosity and Giving Back:** Embrace the concept of giving back and being generous. Acts of kindness and service to others foster a deeper sense of gratitude and connection to the world.

- **Embrace Humility:** Recognize that much of what you are thankful for may not solely be a result of your efforts, but also influenced by the contributions of others and circumstances beyond your control. Embracing humility keeps you grounded in gratitude.

By embodying these principles and consciously practicing gratitude, you will nurture a mindset that enhances your well-being, fosters deeper connections, and allows you to find beauty and joy in the simplest of moments. A gratitude mindset empowers you to lead a more fulfilling and meaningful life, even amidst the challenges that life may bring.

In conclusion, the journey of cultivating a gratitude mindset is an extraordinary odyssey that leads to a profound transformation of your inner world and the way you experience life. As you embrace the principles of gratitude and apply them to your daily life, you open the door to a multitude of positive changes and a deeper connection with the world around you.

Throughout this journey, you have learned to recognize the abundance of blessings that surround you each day. From the simplest joys to the most profound experiences, you have discovered that gratitude holds the key to unveiling the richness of your existence. With patience and persistence, you have nurtured a profound appreciation for the present moment. By practicing mindful presence, you have discovered the beauty of being fully immersed in each experience, free from the burdens of the past and worries about the future.

Through the act of expressing gratitude, you have strengthened your connections with others and deepened your relationships. The genuine appreciation you share has kindled a sense of interconnectedness, fostering a positive and uplifting atmosphere in your social circles.

In the face of challenges and adversity, you have embraced the wisdom of finding silver linings and growth opportunities. You have learned that even amidst difficult times, gratitude can serve as a guiding light, leading you towards resilience and hope.

Moreover, you have discovered the power of self-compassion and the importance of acknowledging your own progress and growth. By extending gratitude to yourself, you have nurtured a kinder and more loving relationship with your own being.

Throughout this journey, you have used visual reminders to anchor yourself in gratitude, creating an environment that encourages and supports your practice. These gentle prompts have served as a constant reminder to appreciate the abundance in your life, no matter how hectic or chaotic it may become.

As you persistently tread upon the path of gratitude, you have celebrated the small victories and embraced the learning curve. You have learned to be patient with yourself, understanding that cultivating a gratitude mindset is a process that unfolds over time.

With each step, you have felt the positive ripple effect of gratitude in your life, touching not only your own heart but also the hearts of those around you. Your genuine expressions of thankfulness have become a beacon of light, inspiring others to embrace the power of gratitude in their own lives.

As you move forward, let gratitude be your constant companion—a source of joy, resilience, and deep contentment. Embrace the magic of thankfulness, and may it continue to open your heart to the countless blessings that surround you. With gratitude as your compass, you embark on a life filled with wonder, appreciation, and a profound connection to the beauty of existence.

CONCLUSION

As we reach the conclusion of this transformative journey, we stand at the precipice of a new understanding—a profound realization that purpose is not a fixed destination, but a dynamic force that intertwines with our lives. Throughout this book, we have delved into the depths of self-discovery, explored the power of authenticity, and embraced the wisdom of change. We have learned to align our values with our actions, connect with others, and find resilience in the face of challenges.

Yet, the journey doesn't end here. Purpose is not a final destination but a lifelong companion—a guiding star that evolves alongside us. It is an ever-unfolding tapestry, woven from the threads of our passions, values, and connections. As we move forward, let us carry the lessons learned and the insights gained, nurturing our purpose with intention and compassion.

Remember that your purpose is unique to you—it may not be grand or dramatic, but it holds immense significance in the tapestry of existence. Embrace your imperfections, for they are the brushstrokes that paint your authentic journey. Cultivate gratitude for every moment, every encounter, and every step along the way.

As you close this book, carry the flame of purpose in your heart, allowing it to illuminate your path even in the darkest of times. Let it guide you, inspire you, and infuse every moment of your existence with a profound sense of meaning and fulfillment.

Remember, you are the author of your own purpose. Embrace the pen, and with every choice you make, with every action you take, write a narrative that echoes with purpose, love, and impact.

Go forth, dear reader, and embark on this beautiful, lifelong journey of finding and nurturing your purpose. The world eagerly awaits the unique gifts only you can offer. For more details on **"How to Find Purpose in Life"** I recommend **"Finding Your purpose"** written by Kathleen Rao. She explains the actual concrete steps to take to determine your specific individual priorities and interests in life.

May this book serve as a constant reminder that purpose is not a destination to be reached but a path to be walked. It is a path that may meander and unfold in unexpected ways, but trust that it will lead you closer to your true self. Embrace the uncertainty, for it is the fertile ground where growth flourishes. Embrace the challenges, for they are the catalysts that shape your character.

RECOMMENDED BOOKS

- **FINDING YOUR PURPOSE:** How to Find Your Purpose In Life and Make the Most of Your Time Here on Earth, a Non-Religious Perspective - (What is the Purpose of Life ?) By Kathleen Rao
- **HOW TO FIND INNER PEACE:** Finding Your Center: (How to Find Inner Peace Through Meditation, Movement, and Self-Reflection.) By Jerry Robert
- **HOW TO DEVELOP A GROWTH MINDSET:** Unleashing Your Potential (A guide to developing a growth mindset.) By Jerry Robert
- **HOW TO BECOME FINANCIALLY INDEPENDENT:** (A comprehensive guide to achieving financial independence and taking control of your finances.) By Jerry Robert
- **DETERMINE TO RAISE:** (How to overcome challenges and achieve success through perseverance and self-determination.) By Jerry Robert

Made in United States
Troutdale, OR
11/27/2024

25398385R00075